TENACITY

How Two Mums Fought
a War on Drugs

GUERNICA WORLD EDITIONS 15

TENACITY

How Two Mums Fought
a War on Drugs

JULIE ROSE,
M.L. & S. J. COWELL

GUERNICA
World
EDITIONS

TORONTO—BUFFALO—LANCASTER (U.K.)
2019

Michael Mirolla, general editor
Scott Walker, editor
Cover design: Allen Jomoc, Jr.
Interior layout: Jill Ronsley, suneditwrite.com
Guernica Editions Inc.
1569 Heritage Way, Oakville, (ON), Canada L6M 2Z7
2250 Military Road, Tonawanda, N.Y. 14150-6000 U.S.A.
www.guernicaeditions.com

Distributors:
University of Toronto Press Distribution,
5201 Dufferin Street, Toronto (ON), Canada M3H 5T8
Gazelle Book Services, White Cross Mills
High Town, Lancaster LA1 4XS U.K.

First edition.
Printed in Canada.

Legal Deposit—Third Quarter
Library of Congress Catalog Card Number: 2018954209
Library and Archives Canada Cataloguing in Publication
Rose, Julie (Julie Ann), author
Tenacity : how two mums fought a war on drugs /
Julie Rose, M.L. & S. J. Cowell.
(Guernica world editions ; 15)

Issued in print and electronic formats.
ISBN 978-1-77183-403-2 (softcover).--ISBN 978-1-77183-404-9
(EPUB).--ISBN 978-1-77183-405-6 (Kindle)

1. Rose, Julie (Julie Ann). 2. Cowell, Marilyn. 3. Parents
of drug addicts--Great Britain--Biography. 4. Mothers and sons--
Great Britain--Biography. 5. Drug addicts--Family relationships--
Great Britain. 6. Biographies. I. Cowell, M. L., author II. Cowell,
S. J., author III. Title. IV. Series: Guernica world editions ; 15

HV4998.R67 2018   362.29092'241   C2018-904699-6
                                                 C2018-904700-3

CONTENTS

Introduction

Although the characteristics of the people in this book are real, the majority of names have been changed to conceal their identity.

Drugs should not be sensationalised. These true life stories depicting factual events were written as a deterrent and information tool. They were produced for the reader to enjoy and reflect upon. They are not necessarily for the addict but to inform those who wouldn't normally sympathise with this subject. They dwell on the emotions, pain and suffering of both mothers and other family members. Hopefully, they have the potential to assist people going through the same ordeal.

Two teenage boys took a wrong turn, leading them to hard drug use, including heroin, with devastating consequences. These two memoirs take you to the depths of a seedy world in an attempt to provide a deeper understanding of the harsh realities of substance abuse. Although primarily focused on drugs, they also deal with the suffering inflicted by alcoholism, gambling and sex addiction. Once a family member is hooked, it becomes an illness that affects everyone without exception.

These memoirs, with flashes of down-to-earth humour amid the tragedy, are examples of triumph over adversity, visions of light amid the darkness. Hence the title: We never gave up despite the odds always being against us.

JULIE'S STORY

CHAPTER ONE

A long way from home ...

Who is Julie Ann Rose? Well, I am just an ordinary person really. Like most, I have had good times and bad times. That's just part of being human, as we are all different but fundamentally the same. When at school I had a passion for music and playing the violin, and thought I would set out to be the best musician I could ever be, but it didn't quite work out that way.

I have been living here in Swindon for the past 43 years. However, it all started in Australia, my birthplace, in 1959.

Before Mum and dad became what were called Ten Pound Poms (people from Britain who immigrated to Australia after the Second World War), they already had a child: my brother, Steven, born in Kingston, London in 1954. Dad was from Feltham, London and my mum, Ann, from Paisley in Scotland. She and her sister, Betty, had a hard upbringing and were abandoned by their father after their mother died in childbirth delivering their younger brother, Patrick. Their father, James Henry McDermott, originated from Southern Ireland but relocated to Scotland, where he met his wife, Janet. After her death, he felt he couldn't cope. So, he placed the girls in a convent in Paisley and sent Patrick off to live with a relative. He relinquished all parental responsibility and joined the navy, partly to distance himself, partly due to finances as work was scarce. The two sisters were raised by Catholic nuns who were strict disciplinarians. There were certainly no frills.

They slept in a dormitory and would get up early every day to carry out their duties of cooking and cleaning. This was alongside their schooling and compulsory praying in the morning, at lunchtime and again before bed. The nuns would ensure they knew their place and that they did as they were told, or there could be harsh consequences.

With no mother and an absent father, what could they look forward to? Mum once told me that she and Betty would wait for hours every Sunday at the convent gates for their father, who had promised to visit. They were let down time and time again because he never showed up, and that feeling of loneliness stayed with her all her life. She never spoke much about what went on there. If I asked, she always avoided the subject, but I knew she was deeply upset at being abandoned from an early age. One thing it did, though, was turn them into survivors who could take care of themselves and hold their own. Many a time, she was picked on but stood up for herself, often resulting in fights with the other girls.

She and Betty left Paisley, aged 17 and 19, and headed down to London, where they found waitressing work at hotels in Richmond. They rented a small flat, which was on the cheap as it was attached to the job, looking after each other as best they could. It was quite an adventure being in the big city and in the middle of everything. They were beginning to live for the first time, experiencing independence and having their own money.

I never knew the whole story regarding mum's background. It was a bit of a mystery which she never fully exposed, so it faded into the past. Let's say she just didn't want to go into detail about it. But that was fine. She was a private person. She would say when asked: "Why do people have to know everything? What has happened to 'mind your own business'?"

My dad, Stanley, a Londoner, was three years younger than mum and had a different background, with a close-knit family. He had two brothers—Donald (Don), the eldest, and John—and a sister, Sue.

Dad, Don and Sue all had the same father, Frank, who was a regimental Sergeant Major at Sandhurst College. Sadly, he died at age 36 from pneumonia in 1937. Not just nursing a broken heart, but because Frank also had been the breadwinner, their mother, Margaret, struggled to feed the children. Uncles and aunties would muck in where they could.

Their motto was to look after your own first and then others. At age nine, Stanley was sent out to bring food back to help feed the family. His mother would tell everyone: "Don't worry. I send Stanley out to bring back the bacon." Stanley started to see himself as the one to rely on, the man of the house, even though he wasn't the eldest son. He kept chickens and made a run so they could have fresh eggs every day, and he would go out to pick fruit and berries. The milkman also noticed a few bottles would go astray from his cart from time to time, but never caught the cheeky culprit.

Eventually their mother remarried to a hardworking, happy go lucky chap called Charlie, who saved the day in many ways. They were able to move to a bigger house, and Margaret and Charlie had a child together, a boy called John, who joined the other three children. Don never accepted Charlie as a replacement father, even though if it weren't for him, god knows what would have happened to them.

Don wouldn't speak two words to Charlie and would threaten Stanley with: "If you ever call him dad, I will knock the shit out of you." Stanley called him dad anyway because he didn't care. He saw Charlie as the saviour and could see he made his mother happy.

Stanley met mum (Ann) in Richmond when he was fresh out of the Royal Marines, after following in his biological father's and brother's footsteps in joining the military. He was a very handsome man: tall and well-built, with thick, black, wavy hair which was swept back, and a hint of olive skin.

He had a lot of charm and confidence and didn't hold back in saying what he wanted to. Overall, I guess you would call him charismatic, and he bore a striking resemblance to the legendary Dean Martin. He first set eyes on Ann when she was dancing at some do one night, wearing quite a short skirt, thinking she had the most amazing legs. He started chatting her up with the mind-set that there is no way this woman would be able to resist him. To his shock she rejected him, even pouring a pint over his head after he pushed his luck once too often. She thought he was only after one thing, so believed that would calm him down. Although stunned, he loved a woman who played hard to get, and she had a lot of fire in her personality. Hence, the start of their passionate relationship.

They married a few years later and had their first child, my older brother, Steven. Dad got a job as a hod carrier, and they were living in a small flat still in Richmond, but they longed for something better. He never got on with the landlord, Mr. Honey, especially after landing him one when he complained about the baby crying all night.

The atmosphere was pretty hostile after that incident, and because he lived in the flat below, they would bump into each other when either going out or coming home. Then one day, out of the blue, Ann got a call from her long-lost brother, Patrick, who had now reached manhood and wanted to meet up as he was coming to London. She would be happy to see him. Although they never really got a chance to have a proper relationship due to circumstances beyond their control, he was her full blood family. The evening didn't quite go as planned, however, as Patrick was not the sweet little brother she had assumed he would be. He was quite the opposite, annoying and arrogant. Most of the night he ignored Ann, which almost seemed deliberate. Instead, he preferred to chat to other people in the pub that he didn't even know, whilst getting drunk on whiskey.

When Stanley saw how his behaviour was upsetting Ann, he couldn't help but to go over to Patrick. He grabbed him by the scruff of the neck and gave him a piece of his mind, but no swinging punches on this occasion. That was the last time they saw Patrick for quite a while.

They didn't have an explanation as to why he acted like this as they had no knowledge of what his childhood consisted of, which may have provided some answers.

Stan and Ann walking along Richmond towpath
with a friend during their courtship.

Prospects were dim, and they couldn't see a future in England as it was difficult to buy your own house with little money. Unsatisfied and searching for something, but not really knowing what, when the Ten Pound Pom scheme was introduced, they jumped at the chance. Paying £10 for travel by sea to Australia, with children going for free, was originally introduced by the British government in 1945. It was created with a view to increase the population of Australia by using Foreign workers to boost industry and get the place on its feet. The heavily subsidised offer was an incentive, but £10 was a lot of money back then, and people struggled to raise it. It was the equivalent of about £375 today, so if you were paying for a couple, a husband and a wife, you were looking at £750.

After initial success, the scheme lay dormant for quite a few years, but its popularity reignited in the late 1950s. The term 'Ten Pound Pom' derives from the cost of the ticket, and the nickname Australians use for the British.

They later dubbed them 'the whinging poms' as they were well known for complaining about anything and everything. The opportunity was finally scrapped in the early 1970s.

* * *

It was very sad for Ann to say goodbye to Betty as they had been through so much together and were soul mates. Betty continued to live in London on the Thames, where she remained for the rest of her life working in the local factory. She married a lovely man named Percy and had one child, a son called Gary, who was the apple of her eye and brought her great joy.

Frank Fowler, Stanley's father.

CHAPTER TWO

S tanley, Ann and Steven boarded the *Castel Felice* for a six-week sail to Australia, mum being five months pregnant at the time with my second brother, Mark. The British government promised good prospects through this scheme, but it wasn't quite like that when you got there. On arrival in the state of Victoria, they were placed in a hostel in Melbourne, which is where they remained until after my birth a few years later. Living with three children under these conditions was difficult as in the late 1950s there were no hand-outs or help.

However, sometime later, the opportunity to reinvent themselves arose. Dad was a builder by trade, so he seized the offer of purchasing some cheap land. With his own hands, he built a weatherboard house, and this was the beginning of a new and different life. My sister, Maggie, came later in 1965, so the three of us were Australian-born. The tropical weather and the outdoor life was beautiful for us kids; it was paradise to say the least. We would eat breakfast on the veranda, swim every day after school, and go pony riding. I remember staying up late sometimes when we would all be outside in the warm air and just laying on my back on the grass. I would stare up at the night sky which was full of thousands of shimmering stars, like diamonds. This was the most amazing sight I have ever seen. Daytime was hot, oh god it was hot, and the saying "you can fry an egg on the pavement" is true. I loved it, everything about it. It was all I knew. It was part of me and still is to this day.

There were hard times too, as Australia is a tough country, depending on where you are situated. But if you didn't work, you didn't eat.

However, it was a journey my parents wouldn't have missed as it teaches you so much, and it enables you to use your own resources. It certainly made mum and dad grow up with a bang. During this period, Dad was working seven days a week, meaning mum was at home coping with four children alone. Therefore, the pressure was on, albeit a different type of pressure than we have today.

One hot day, I was running after our dog, Tuppy, who was heading towards the road outside of our house. The roads weren't made of tarmac; they were just an exposed, rocky surface. Dad dashed after me to stop me from harm as he saw danger, but in doing that he fell to the ground, breaking his ribs and leaving him strapped up for weeks. It was hot and dusty, so you had to be tough to take it.

Tragedy struck again when he got involved in a car accident one night when travelling home from work with his buddy, Dick. Dick was driving, and he suddenly smashed into a tree, catapulting dad through the windscreen so that he hit his head full force. He was hospitalized for weeks and feared to have brain damage, but thankfully he managed to pull through. How he survived that I will never know.

Mum being solitary all day, apart from us four and the flies, took its toll. On more than one occasion, she would head down the road with her suitcase spluttering: "I can't do this anymore!" It all got too much, and dad would have to run after her and bring her back. Apart from loving her so much, there was no way he could work and look after us on his own. I never understood at the time why she did this, but now that I am older, I do understand how she felt.

During my childhood, as the eldest daughter, I was always around my mum, who wore some lovely clothes. Her attire of classy dresses, sun glasses, black hair and slender figure reminded me of the elegant Jackie Kennedy. Mum certainly looked the part as she was beautiful, and I really was in awe of her, although she was fairly strict and didn't stand for any nonsense. We were sometimes treated to a posh restaurant for seafood, and for these occasions she would put me in a lovely, girly dress, usually pink or blue because she loved those colours, along with black patent shoes and pure white ankle socks. I had long, thick blonde hair which she would tie up in a silk ribbon, especially when we went out somewhere special. She loved to show me off to everyone, which gave me a lot of confidence.

One of my parents' worst experiences was when I vanished from Frankton beach, age six. We went there for a day trip, along with my two brothers, running around having fun. Mum and dad left instructions for Mark and Steven to look after me whilst they went off to get lunch. My brothers started fighting. I got worried, so I wandered off, but not towards my parents. I went in the opposite direction of Seaford beach, five miles away. I was totally lost, but I just kept walking. As time went on, it started to get dark. Mum and dad were frantic and alerted the Aussie police, who were searching for me in helicopters, scanning the beaches below. The coast guards actually said they hoped the sharks hadn't eaten me for dinner.

I was very frightened, but walked aimlessly on under the beating sun, which was now burning me quite badly. The few people who were around didn't take any notice of me, and at this point my legs felt like lumps of lead. I didn't anticipate making it back safely, which is a feeling I can remember to this day. It never leaves you. When the police eventually picked me up, I was scared like a lost sheep and exhausted.

Even they were astounded by the distance I had covered, which took from daybreak to dusk, being so young and small. It's a wonder they found me at all. I was returned to my mum, who was pregnant with my sister, Maggie, at the time and in a right state. Her face was red, and tears were streaming down. She was crying uncontrollably, and I thought she was going to collapse on the spot. Dad, on the other hand didn't look too happy. Although relieved, I could sense his anger.

Mum and the boys at home in rural Melbourne.

* * *

(The following is an account in Stanley's own words)

I landed in Melbourne, Victoria on 11 December 1956 with my wife Ann and eldest son Steven, hoping for the best. We were on a coach heading for Nunawading, a town on the outskirts of the city, which passed an open truck carrying the biggest vegetables I have ever seen. It was explained to me later that root veg grew to such a size in the search for water which was often lacking.

The carrots must have been 18 inches long, which taught me one thing: Life is going to be tough here judging by the hard ground. I knew that as I was in the construction industry.

The hostel was composed of about one hundred huts in the middle of a small forest, with one hut accommodating three to six family members. I loved it; my Ann hated it! It was communal eating in a large cafeteria, and the food was dished out onto your plate as you queued with your tray. Meals were free until you were working and could pay your own way, which they expected to be about two weeks after arriving. The setting bought back memories of my old military barracks. The facilities were good and the main thing I appreciated is that hot water was always available for when you wanted to use one of the many showers or baths. We all shared washing lines and it was a god send to be able to get your laundry dry within minutes thanks to the sweltering climate. The place also hosted an indoor cinema and because we were only down the road from the beach that was how you amused yourself during your time there.

It wasn't just Brits that were immigrating. There were many families from Germany, Italy and Holland as the scheme was also promoted by their governments. Aussie men outnumbered women in the hundreds so females were spoilt for choice. A lot of the newcomers found they were single shortly after being in the country as their wives deserted them in favour of the Aussie charm and masculinity. Ann, who was heavily pregnant with our second son, was on the verge of packing up and going home, but soon after was taken to Box Hill hospital, to give birth.

Work came my way and there was plenty of it due to a shortage of bricklayers so was earning great money and told her it wouldn't be long before we could buy some land and build a house. In the meantime I decided to teach her how to drive, so bought her a small car, to get around. She loved the independence and every afternoon she would take the kids to the beach, which was ten miles long. That put a smile on her face and I thought I should take a photo to capture the moment.

In the fifties Australia had a white policy, which was criticized all over the world. The prime minister's philosophy which he reiterated to other world leaders was: "This is our country and we will govern it the way we see fit." You were liable to pay for your own medical bills, but to help towards the cost you could pay into a fund or get cheap insurance which would cover 80% of the overall amount. Dental treatment, school books, pens, and pencils were also your own responsibility but again there were other schemes to subsidise this. You paid your own way, and I personally found myself better off, rather than making weekly national insurance contributions.

The way of life out there meant the first thing you needed was a large fridge so to always have an ice-cold beer on hand. Secondly was a decent car, which cost next to nothing to fill it up. It was cheaper than the UK as you could even get half a sheep for a couple of quid. The Aussies are tough; you have to be to endure the summer heat when laying bricks, and even they themselves say: "This country isn't made for us." I think they were implying the conditions are more suitable for the black fellas (Aborigines) who are the original inhabitants and have the genetic makeup to be able to withstand it.

It was a young land and to my belief it had risen from out of the sea first as there is no top soil. You have to spend a tenner for a five yard truck load of mountain soil a few times over to cover your area. The timber comes from the red gum tree, and it is very heavy and strong; hence the reason it is used to build houses.

The bricks are then wrapped around it, which is called black veneer. Every home is individually designed and was something you expect to see in a fairy tale book. Two carpenters would erect the building in just six days, including the roof, walls, windows and doors. In fact, due to the hard labour the life span of a carpenter out there was only 45–50 years of age.

I remember one day after work in a place called Mount Waverly there was an old couple who accidentally drove their car two wheels down a ditch at the side of the road. They started to panic, then, luckily a truck pulled up and four to five Aussies jumped out and said: "Don't worry old timers we'll get you out." They proceeded to lift the car, with the couple still in it and pulled them back on the road, no trouble! One of them put his head through the window and said to the old man: "You drive straight home now, no drinking you old bastard."

This was the attitude of the Aussie male, just get stuck in and sort it, no messing. They then all walked into the pub laughing as I followed them in for a pint with my mate, Joe Craig. Joe was an Aussie but originated from Irish stock. He provided the transport after buying a new Vauxhall car, even teaching me how to drive as well as the finer points of bricklaying. He was a lovely bloke with brown hair and wore a clean trilby hat, but at only five feet three inches tall he was an easy target for the butt of the Aussie male jokes.

They singled him out to pick on, mainly having a laugh about his unfortunate height. In those times women were not allowed in the public bar area and it was a bare setting with no seating just a pool table in the middle of the floor. Every Friday night after a long hard week at work, without fail there would be a punch up as the blokes would be vented up from working the last five days in blistering heat. That's how it got you. Women who were referred to as 'Sheilas' could sit in a separate area called 'The Ladies Lounge' kitted out with tables and chairs, providing their husbands were present. Females weren't allowed to go up and buy their own drinks but due to human right activists fighting against sex segregation in bars the policy came to an end in the mid 1970s.

There was a lot to learn but I embraced it and loved my new way of life. Apart from the training Joe Craig had given me the rest I picked up from my earlier days on site as a hod carrier. I always wanted to progress but there was never any money to achieve qualifications as whatever I earned was all about using it to survive. Nearly three years after arriving, my daughter Julie was born, with her blonde hair and blue eyes. It was quite a shock as I had two ginger haired sons, so thought me and Ann must do it in a certain way! Or was there something I didn't know about!

My first motor was an American Ford Custom Line 30 HP, big enough to carry us all in comfort, not to mention our dog, Tuppy. I was eligible for a loan of £850 from the ANZ Bank, which was classed as a lot of money back then and enough for a plot of land. I became the proud owner of a quarter of an acre in Forest Hills, making a deal with a carpenter; him to do the frame and I would do the brickwork myself. In a short space of time the house was ready and we all moved in.

It had open plan design, allowing plenty of space for the kids, who were all growing up fast, with Julie now being six, and as beautiful as ever. One afternoon we went to Frankton beach, Ann being pregnant with our youngest child, Ann Margaret, but we called her Maggie, after my mother. She had hair as black as ebony, and what with Julie being as blonde as they come, then two red heads, my children were real dolly mixtures. We left the kids on the beach whilst me and Ann went across the road to bring back lunch for them, with strict instructions to Mark and Steven, to look after Julie. We weren't gone long, only to return and find the two boys fighting and Julie nowhere in sight! Initially I felt anger at the lads for not keeping an eye on her, then drafted in fellow beachgoers to join the search. After no luck I called in the coast guard and the police. They told us to stay put as they would find her, and the next thing we noticed was the helicopters and sniffer dogs. I thought 'that's it' either the sharks have had her or some weirdo has snatched her.

Ann was in a terrible state and at her wits' end, which wasn't needed in her condition. To our relief the police found her walking on the beach, having covered a five mile stretch looking for us. She was crying her eyes out and shaking all over. I felt like strangling the two boys but getting her back was thankful enough.

After this episode I finished the house off, constructing a high patio with 12 ft. long windows, so we could turn the TV round and watch it from the outside. The evenings were lovely so with the help of a few cold beers and lemonade for the kids, we could watch the sunset, which was twice as big here and blood red. It really was the best time of the day.

My days were hard so when I finished work at about 1–2 pm, because it was so hot, I would go home to Ann who always had some cold tins in the fridge. I would sit down in the cool shower, letting the water wash over me as I was knackered, to say the least. My advice to people, even now, is don't sit in that sun, always cover up and protect yourself. Otherwise it will make you very ill. Skin cancer appears to be quite high in Australia, but the real Aussie won't sunbathe for long periods of time.

In November in the 1960s in the state of Victoria we were drifting towards a very hot summer, with a hose ban already imposed. Anyone seen throwing a lit butt out of the car window was fined $200 on the spot. The potential danger of a bush fire would be disastrous for both the families and the wildlife. It could cause a stampede as the animals would fear for their lives, which we witnessed sooner than we thought. A few days later we were faced with a fire on a 60 mile front, which was heading our way. The alarm went out for volunteers to help fight the crisis and I enlisted, along with some of my buddies.

Fire brigades arrived from other states with concrete trucks filled with water, trying to stem the impossible task. A Fire Chief shouted: "We will stop the fire on this wide road." But the flames in the tall trees exploded through the heat and leapt across the road to the forest on the other side. If the oxygen around us had ignited we would have all perished. One thing I learned about Mother Nature is when she decides to do something nothing will stand in her way. After three days, exhausted, we were on the ground and unable to speak through the smoke and fire, as all the moisture was zapped from our bodies.

The scene around us looked like the end of the world, with everything burnt, black and very dry. Thankfully most of the residents managed to escape, although we lost some families when attempting to put out their burning homes, without hope. Fortunately, our house remained untouched but my prayers went out to the dead folk and animals.

On the way back from the catastrophe me and the blokes stumbled across an old pub, which the owner kept open for the firefighters. To neck down a refreshing cold beer which was laid on for free was a surreal moment as we were lucky to be alive. However out of it one discovered strength, companionship and a sense of achievement. I will never forget that fire: You can't win. It keeps going until there is nothing left to burn.

The Melbourne Cup was getting close and it is the only country in the world to have a national day off for a horse race, which was great. My mates and I backed a couple of winners, whilst drinking a lot of beer and eating plenty of pies, the best I ever tasted. We left this one pub to go to another, which had just opened and was on the way home. The White Horse Hotel, consisted of two bars and two dance floors, something we weren't used to in Nunawading, 17 miles from the nearest city. I asked the leader of the band if I could sing along to the music they were playing, to which he agreed. When finished I received a few claps and was happy until the bouncer approached and told me to leave the premises. I took one look at his big frame and realised it was me that got us into this situation through no fault of my own. The Aussie himself doesn't like to lose, so when he followed me outside, he had all his sidekicks with him. They were actually off-duty police officers earning themselves some extra cash by working for the club, (moonlighting) which was in fact illegal.

The big guy came up to me and began poking his finger in my chest, whilst saying: "Don't come back here again pom or you will have me to deal with." Seeing myself as a bit of a wide boy, my response was: "No thanks. We will deal with it right now." And with that I threw my best right hook, landing on his great big nose. He went face down like a sack of shit and I knew he was really hurt. His partners in crime then jumped on me and gave me the mother of all beatings, making sure they never hit me where it showed.

My ribs were broken and my knees were badly swollen, but when the police arrived they just chucked me in the back of the wagon. One of the psycho officers mounted me, injuring my back when slapping on the handcuffs, before driving me to Blackburn nick for the cells. This police station was the one used to remand Ronnie Biggs, The

Great Train Robber, after he was captured in Australia. He fled to the country after scaling over the walls of Wandsworth prison in London, but his incarceration at Blackburn was short-lived because there was no security, the jail mimicked a bungalow housing a couple of cells and the place was easy to just walk out of.

Detective Sergeant Adams was in Box Hill hospital lying in a coma and if he didn't come out of it I would not be leaving the police station. I could even be facing a murder rap. I should have called Ann to let her know what was going on but I couldn't handle her wrath on top of the trouble I was already in.

A few days later, to my blessing, he aroused to consciousness so the seriousness of the charge lessened and I was released. The wife picked me up after being eventually informed of my whereabouts and we drove home in silence. When the shock wore off she commented that my shirt was all torn and covered in blood.

I knew I could be looking at a long stretch in prison as they already stated the case would be going up for prosecution and I didn't feel good about the outcome. At this point I knew I needed to get some legal assistance, so managed to get an appointment with a barrister of law in Melbourne city. After a few meetings, at $90 a shot, I was given the bare faced facts, of why I couldn't win. As the man is a police officer, I would be looking at two years minimum in jail.

Two years!! There is no way I could leave Ann and the children to fend for themselves for that length of time. There would be no dough coming in so how would they survive? No, I had to think on my feet and make a quick decision, however hard it was to swallow, as I loved this place. We got a cancellation booking on an Italian cruise liner as I thought: If we're going back, then we're doing it in style.

One cool evening under the blanket of the midnight sky we packed up our things, loaded them into the car and headed for the port. The ship was a beauty. With her gleaming white bodywork and black trim, she was a sight for sore eyes. Her deck boosted a swimming pool and cinema and the sleeping arrangements were two separate cabins, one for the parents whilst the kids all bunked together in the other. Food was included in the cost of the ticket which was £2,000 in today's money for the whole family to travel. We went the long way round, firstly sailing to New Zealand and then onto Tahiti. Boy, did we visit some of the most beautiful countries on the planet. When docking at the Cape of Good Hope, a young man I had been chatting with on the journey disembarked in order to do some shopping.

I don't know how it happened but he got stabbed and killed. Immediately I thought of his family in England whom he hadn't seen for years, telling me this during our conversation. It was very sad and I couldn't get it out of my mind for ages. We continued on to South America, travelling through the Panama Canal and Acapulco, where we watched the cliff divers at La Quebrada, the site of their famous performance. Since 1934 this has been one of Mexico's feature attractions as divers leap from 136 ft. cliffs, crashing into an 11 ft. deep inlet in the Pacific. They give five performances daily, including four evening shows with the divers having to carry torches—an unforgettable spectacle as meditation and prayer are part of the routine. Next was to Lisbon, Portugal before finally arriving at Southampton, England and guess what? It was raining! I then turned and said to Ann: "What do you think, shall we go back to the sun again?" No comment!

*Dad, brother Steven and mum
about to set sail.*

Steven, myself and Mark.

The hostel we lived for a while in Nunawading.

CHAPTER THREE

That was the end of our Australian adventure as that evening we set off and slowly sailed out to sea away from the Australian coast. That scene would be forever etched in my mind, even though being only nine years old at the time.

I stood at the stern of the ship watching the country I grew up in fading away into the sunset, not knowing whether I would ever see it again. This was a new chapter in my life, and I wondered what lay ahead for me. I didn't feel fear as it was exciting like an adventure, but somehow I sensed this shouldn't be happening.

We were on board that ship for six weeks, and what an adventure it was seeing all those amazing destinations. I can remember running up and down the decks when we were at sea, and at night I would sneak up to the bow of the ship. I would watch the waves crashing in the rough Indian Ocean whilst standing upon the rails, just like in the film *Titanic*. I shouldn't have been there really as it was dangerous. I could have easily fallen overboard in a split second.

At Southampton, all of dad's family were waiting to greet us at the port. As we had nowhere to go straight away, we needed their help. Mum, dad, myself and Maggie were to stay with John, dad's younger half-brother, in a terraced council house in Swindon. It was going to be a tight squeeze as he had two kids himself. My brothers were sent to live temporarily with our grandmother, Margaret, and step-granddad, Charlie. They were part of the 'London Overflow', people who wanted to move from the over-populated outskirts of the city.

Things were great for a while, but mum and John's wife, Vera, didn't always see eye to eye. And as they were both confrontational characters, sparks would fly. One day they came to blows over the children squabbling, which involved Vera's son and Maggie.

He pushed Maggie down the stairs and hurt her quite badly, so mum slapped him as she was having none of it. Vera retaliated, and they ended up having a cat fight, both receiving scratches all over their faces. Dad got between them to intervene, and after that incident the atmosphere was tense, as you can well imagine.

Counteracting the episode, John, who suffered from asthma, endured a very bad attack shortly afterwards and collapsed on the living room floor. Luckily, mum had just re-entered the house from shopping and revived him by opening his airways and doing chest compressions. She called the ambulance, and when the medics arrived to assess the situation, they said her actions had saved his life. Following the event, mum and Vera found some common ground, although the peaceful environment was short-lived when John, a Driving Instructor, was caught out having an affair. Apparently, it had been going on for quite some time, under her nose, and it was with one of his driving pupils.

When Vera found out, she dealt with it the only way she knew how: by swinging her best right hook, straight in his face. He went down on the kitchen floor like a sack of shit! I remember coming in from school and seeing a pair of feet sticking out from the kitchen door; it was John out cold. A little while later, Vera said she was going out for a packet of ciggies. She never returned.

She left the children with John, who then went on to marry Brenda, the woman he had been having an affair with.

Whilst staying at John's, I attended the local school and got teased for my Aussie accent. I disliked the kids because they didn't take to me as I was different, and they were unsure how to react to me, this foreigner. At the time, I thought they looked scruffy compared to the kids at my old school, who were well turned out and organised. Deep down, I started to feel loneliness in my new surroundings. It was a huge transition for me as there was no swimming in the lovely ocean every day or open spaces to run around in.

I felt like the odd one out and can only liken my situation to being an ocean fish in a stream.

Even mum felt depressed. Although she moaned about Australia, it was a case of realising what she had and now lost. She came back only to find it wasn't the England she once knew, which mirrored many other Ten Pound Poms. After returning to their homeland and finding it not all that, they would go back to Oz and would be known as the Boomerang Poms.

After nearly a year at John's, it was time to move on because it was only temporary, and the fact the two boys were placed separately wasn't ideal. My parents scraped a deposit together and could just about afford the monthly rent on a private house, meaning the family could be together again. It was located in a quiet part of Swindon. To economise, instead of hiring help to move, my dad transported our stuff in a borrowed black hearse-type vehicle.

Approximately six months after moving in, we were provided with a council house, a three-bed end terrace in Walcot, where dad still lives today after 40 years plus. I looked at the terraced houses in our new street and thought they were so small, only big enough to be apartments, as properties in Australia are so much bigger. However, there is so much more land in that vast country. The double-decker buses were a novelty, as I only ever had seen single floor vehicles previously. Two things that did put me on a downer were the grey skies and the rain, which took a lot of getting used to over the years.

I was trying to find a connection to my new life, so I joined the Girl Guides, and rediscovered my interest in music. When I was twelve, I learnt how to play the violin at school and became quite good. My teacher even commented that he had never heard anyone play like me at such a young age. He was so impressed that he put me forward to play for the Swindon Orchestra and local theatre, where I finally made friends, with people I had more in common with, and it felt great. By the time I had reached 14, I had turned into the blonde, slim one at senior school. I was shy but knew the boys liked me, although I was more interested in my music, which is what stood between me and everyone else.

However, as a teenager, other things got in the way as we were young and discovering. The different types of music certainly dominated the era, with people hitting the dance floor at the discos. We tried to be older than we were by drinking cheap cider without mums and dads finding out. The violin took a back seat for quite a while after that.

One of my new pals was a girl called Helen, who was three years older than me and from a large Irish family. She was quite a stunner with her thick brown hair and beautiful Celtic looks, including the traditional green emerald eyes. We used to muck about together over by the canal, but as she was the eldest in her family, a lot of her time was taken with looking after the younger siblings. You could sense she wanted something better from her life; it was like she was always searching.

The canal was a quiet area surrounded by greenery and tall trees, a pretty setting although the water was murky. We would spend time there jumping from bank to bank trying not to fall in and go apple noggin, even experimenting sharing drags on our first cigarettes. Despite the peacefulness, the place was plagued by an infamous flasher whom we had the misfortune to meet. We ran for dear life after seeing this guy in his twenties with his trousers down to his ankles exposing his meat and two veg. I didn't understand what he was doing at the time, but he was masturbating vigorously. Not something you want to see when out pinching a bit of fruit.

My other friend, a guy named Jeremy, was completely different. He was a hairdresser, five years my senior. He was six feet tall with naturally dark hair, which he dyed peroxide blonde and cut into a feathered style finished off wispy at the bottom. He was a smoker with skin that tanned very easily, always wearing tight trousers to enhance his assets as he did have an attractive physique. He would do my hair for me as well as my mum's, who loved him and vice versa as he relished the company of women. There was just one problem for Jeremy: He was gay, which was so detectable with his camp voice and female tendencies, and being gay in the 1970s was not socially accepted.

Dad wasn't best pleased with me hanging around with him as I was impressionable, so he was trying to protect me. However, his advice didn't sway me, and I hung around with Jeremy anyway as he was creative and funny, qualities I craved. His family were also part of the London overflow, which was another reason that we clicked.

Trouble is, he was always being picked on by other guys. One time he was trapped in a red phone box, too petrified to come outside and face the gang of thugs waiting to attack him. He took advantage of having a phone to hand and called my dad for help, saying: "Stan come up here quick. They are going to kill me!" Dad came to his rescue, and as soon as the bullies saw him they scarpered.

As much as I liked Jeremy, there was another side to him that I didn't want to be on the receiving end of. He could be very catty, and shockingly he could take it to levels I never thought him capable of. Our mutual friend Wendy and he fell out over something very trivial which had happened in the past. It was later resolved, but Jeremy had other plans. He offered to colour her hair at his home, which she gladly accepted as she was always experimenting with different shades. But his intentions were not honourable. When her time was up for the bleach to be washed out, she looked in the mirror, and to her horror he had turned her hair green! Secretly he had been harbouring a grudge since their dispute and took his revenge when she was least expecting it, ruining her crown and glory. She ran home crying to her parents, who were so incensed to see what Jeremy had done on purpose that they marched around to his house and started banging on the door. I guess he was a coward, unable to face the music, and he just ignored their knocks, hoping they would eventually go away.

I suspected his bitchiness derived from a long-running feud he had with his father that had damaged him and caused his behaviour to be unstable. Since I had known Jeremy, his father had always been ill, bed-ridden and surviving on just one lung, reliant on an oxygen tank. He was very vocal in expressing his unacceptance of his son's sexuality. In retaliation, Jeremy would shout up "die, you bastard" with real venom, when his father called out from his bed. I didn't really take it seriously at the time. I thought it was just some kind of joke between them.

The hatred between them was deep-rooted, although he did have a good rapport with his mother. She was a lovely woman, a chain smoker known for wearing a multi-coloured head scarf knotted at the front.

Another person to feel Jeremy's wrath, with much worse consequences, was the owner of the salon where he was working as second in charge. After they had got involved in a disagreement, Jeremy took it upon himself to enter the salon at night, as he was a key holder, and start a fire by lighting a match to the place. The owner turned up for work the next morning only to find his livelihood burnt to the ground, and he was distraught to say the least.

The arsonist was never caught, and soon after his wicked deed, Jeremy relocated to London, which is when I lost contact with him. I did, however, bump into him later in life and saw that his appearance had completely changed as he was bald and overweight. Losing his hair was something I always warned him of due to his constant bleaching. The other thing I found surprising was that, by the time he reached the age of 38, he had married a woman. I don't know whether he was always bisexual, or he just switched. Notwithstanding his faults, Jeremy was a talented stylist and makeup artist who went on to work with high-profile stars in a top salon.

He lived in a dream world most of the time and escaped to a place where no one could reach him. Perhaps he was there when committing those nasty acts and not in comprehension of what he was doing, or maybe he had a split personality.

CHAPTER FOUR

It was the '70s era, and as teenagers we were into pop music and the opposite sex. We didn't know much about sexual relationships as it wasn't part of education. And as I was quite reserved, it was more about curiosity. When I was sixteen, I managed to get an apprenticeship at a hairdresser in the town centre, allowing me to branch out and expand my social circle. One evening, I went out with Wendy and met Dave, who was 17 and worked as a roof tiler. I didn't think much of him at first, but he had this presence about him, and shortly after we began dating. He got a job on site at the John Murray Building, which coincidentally was near my salon. I wanted to see him all the time as I was now beginning to fall for him, even using my lunch break to wander down to the site. On a hot summer's day, I would stand on the concrete below and gaze up at the skyscraper in progress, hoping to catch a glimpse of him. After noticing, he would venture down towards me, topless and exposing his tanned and muscular physique. Wow, talk about a six pack! He wasn't blessed with height but was fit and attractive to a lot of girls, and didn't he half know it.

The majority of young men around this period went in for a trade such as building, carpentry, plumbing and labouring, the more manual type of role. As Swindon was up and coming, in fact branded the fastest growing town in Europe, most males I knew worked in these fields. They worked hard and played hard, which is what has made the town it is today. Many of our ground workers originated from Ireland and turned out to be very successful over the years, doing what they did.

Dave took me by storm, in a nutshell, and everything just seemed to happen so quickly with him. He had an aura about him exuding a

30

dominant character and an element of danger. Maybe I was so drawn to him because he resembled the men in our family, who are strong-minded. I have to say, I prefer men who are a bit rough around the edges.

I had to keep him secret initially as dad would have hit the roof if he were aware. He knew of Dave and wasn't impressed. It was understandable as Dave was a challenge and spoke his mind. So, people either liked him or didn't. He could be controlling and wanted his own way, which I went along with because I wanted to be with him. Being innocent, I lost myself in the relationship and fell passionately in love with him, hating it when we were apart. Dad was never totally happy about my relationship with Dave. I started to feel I was slipping from that pedestal he had put me on.

Our love was stronger than ever, and I married Dave anyway. It was 1976. I was 17, and he was 19. We had a church wedding, and I wore a white dress as mum was traditional and wouldn't have it any other way. Jeremy did a good job of my hair and makeup, and I felt like a princess. Dad paid for the whole day, even putting money behind the bar at the Piccadilly pub, ensuring everyone had a great time. The majority of the guests were from Swindon, including the many tradesmen we knew, and dad's family from London. I invited my friend Helen, but to my surprise she never showed up, and her absence bothered me throughout the day. Once the celebrations were over, we returned to Dave's mum's large bungalow with its huge grounds. As we didn't have a house yet, Dave's mum and dad made their caravan at the bottom of her garden available. It was an old, white caravan with an open-plan living area.

To sleep, we would pull the couch out. There was a hob and cooker which ran on bottled gas and was good enough to be able to roast a full chicken, which I can recall doing quite often with smoke pouring out of every gap.

It did have its own toilet, but to take a shower I would have to wear my dressing gown up to the bungalow, before getting dressed and coming back again. We were welcome in the main house anytime and would pop up to have cups of tea and a chat, but I always loved returning to the caravan for our privacy. My dad was astonished I was living in a caravan as he always expected something better for me, but I was happy there. I was crazy in love, and made it homey by placing our wedding photos in any space available.

My excitement at being a married lady was slightly marred as my thoughts were consumed by Helen, and my disappointment in her. The next morning, I got up full of beans and made my way to my parents' home, both of whom had sullen faces when I arrived. My dad was sitting in his chair, quiet and looking down at the floor. So, I said: "What's wrong?" thinking, we have just had a wedding. "It's me, your daughter." I knew he wasn't pleased about me getting married so young, but this was something different, Then he told me: "Helen is dead."

I just stood there in shock; I couldn't take it in as he proceeded to say she was killed in a car crash the night before. Apparently, she was last seen getting into a car with three young guys on their way to Lambourne, Berkshire. They were suspected of drinking, or at least the driver had a few and crashed the vehicle on a country road. Poor Helen went straight through the windscreen, landing up in the next field, dying instantly at the tender age of 21.

She loved listening to Gilbert O'Sullivan. I will always remember that about her. I didn't know how to feel as it was the first time I experienced a death, but both sadness and anger overwhelmed me. If she had come to my wedding, she might still be alive today.

After the tragedy, I couldn't sleep at night and kept waking up seeing her in my bedroom trying to talk to me. Maybe she was, or perhaps it was just my imagination. I don't know. She was so young, and I felt the pain. Her mother was beside herself with grief as you would imagine.

It wasn't long before I fell pregnant and had my daughter, Tilly, who was born nine weeks premature. I went into labour very quickly, and they couldn't stop the contractions, so she only weighed three pounds, 12 ounces and was just like a little doll with dark hair and big blue-green eyes. She had to stay in hospital for seven weeks until her weight reached five pounds, and it was very hard not being able to take my baby home like other mothers. However, that is the way it was, and I accepted it as I was just thankful that she was healthy and could begin to grow. Every day I would venture up to the premature baby unit to see her and stay for the whole day.

As I was unable to hold her, I had to make do with putting my hands through the round holes in the side of the incubator to touch and stroke her. This wasn't a natural start for mother and baby, but nevertheless we were making our own special bond. She knew who I was and would drink the milk I expressed that the nurses fed her, who would comment on how strong she was. Despite her fragile beginning, she went on to be a wholesome baby, and is now a very healthy adult without suffering any illnesses because of being premature.

We were still living in the caravan. It was January 1977, and so cold, and the snow seemed to go on forever. The accommodation was not suitable for a delicate newborn. It had lost its charm. At night she and I would have to go up to the bungalow to sleep as there were plenty of spare rooms. Although Dave's mum did offer, it was my responsibility to do the night feeds, and as I had already spent too much time away from her, I wouldn't have had it any other way. The situation worked well as it was a large family, and everyone mucked in. Dave's sister was a nursery nurse, so she was very keen to put herself forward for the occasional babysitting and help with the laundry.

Dave was generally a lively person who was up one minute and down the next, and he was volatile without any pre-warning. Although exciting to be around, he had an annoying habit of kicking off at the least thing. I guess that's why we had a love-hate relationship. His first reaction to a challenging situation would be to let rip without thinking things through. Hence, after a night out with the boys, an iron came flying through the caravan window. I was never sure what that was all about, but something crazy always seemed to be happening.

* * *

We finally came to the top of the list for a council house and were given a three-bed terrace in a cul-de-sac, close to the local primary school. I was in my comfort zone as many of the other residents were young married couples with kids. An added bonus was that a lot of them were London overflows, a connection to my roots.

No one had much money then, but they were all great characters and hard-working people, with the men always looking for employment. Our homes couldn't have been cleaner, and a lot of us housewives would scrub our doorsteps with bleach, and even the pavement in the garden. It seemed we were all cut from the same cloth. The thing I loved the most is that we all helped each other. So, if we needed something, even as simple as a cup of sugar, it wouldn't be frowned upon. Quite regularly, we would do an exchange: a few slices of bread for a bit of washing powder, and anyone would be welcome to use your lawn mower if you were lucky enough to own one.

We were all in the same boat. It wasn't about keeping up with the Joneses, and I liked the concept that you could turn to a neighbour without being portrayed as a scrounger. As time has moved on, we have more in terms of material things, but we seemed to have lost the great community spirit or have much less than we had years ago. Most will admit they don't even know their neighbour, and gone are the friendly chats over the garden fence.

On the estate, the local Del Boy was a geezer called Mac. He was the person to see if you ever needed anything, which was usually stuff off the back of a lorry. As most people didn't have much money, Mac could get them anything knock-off, from cheap booze to a car or a sofa. But as Dave had his own resources and was a grafter, our family never went without. Mac was a short chap with dark hair and resembled a character out of *The Godfather*, almost like he should have lived in another time. Everyone liked him with his laid-back attitude as he was an unassuming guy who never passed judgement.

Years before he had been in an accident which required him to receive a blood transfusion, only the blood he was given was infected with hepatitis B, a virus which destroys the liver.

From then on, he slowly became very ill to the point that he needed a liver transplant, which kept him going for many years. However, the replacement liver began to show signs of deterioration. Then one day he suffered internal bleeding and was rushed to a specialist hospital in Oxford. They tried to save his life; but, sadly, Mac died on a hot August day age 42, leaving a wife and two children. Our loveable rogue Del Boy was gone, and everyone was devastated.

CHAPTER FIVE

In 1978, I went full-term with my second baby and gave birth to a little boy whom we named Scott. What a handsome little chap with gorgeous blonde curls and blue eyes. He must have inherited my set of genes. The four of us were very happy in our little house. We weren't blessed materially, but my marriage was thriving, and we had these two lovely little babies, so we were fulfilled. To express our joy, Dave and I would go out dancing. We loved Womack & Womack's 'Teardrops' song, an 80s classic, as well as The Bee Gees, who also were renowned for being Ten Pound Poms. We had a great time and would go on holiday to Spain with Dave's brother, Pete, and his wife, Sandra. We all hit it off like a house on fire. God, we had some good times with them, but every now and then a voice in my head would be saying: "I would love all of us to move to Australia and live the dream." I would discuss this sometimes with Dave, but he never took it very well. In his mind, it must have been too big a step.

Tilly and Scott were so different. She was feistier like Dave, and Scott more sensitive like me. Nevertheless, they were close. Sometimes they would get on, and sometimes they wouldn't, just like most normal kids. As they started to blossom, their individual personalities came to the fore, with Tilly being a little shy but clever. As there were only 19 months between them, and no matter how much love you show the first one, this new little baby stole her space for a while. My curly haired boy, an inquisitive soul, full of energy and happy, who made friends easily. I never had any problems with them as they were both well-behaved.

I cherished my time at home with them and hated anyone else looking after them apart from mum as this was my duty. After enrolling in primary school, Scott was forever bringing a chum back with him at the end of the day. He was particularly friendly with a little boy called Simon, who was a quiet and shy boy who came from a family in the next street. He had wispy fair hair and hazel eyes and was one of five. He had been born with one leg shorter than the other, but that only added to my affection for him.

Simon's home was troublesome as his father, Ray, was a hard worker but also a drunk, and after a heavy session would unleash his frustrations on his wife. One night, we had settled down watching the TV. Just before going to bed, we were startled by screams in conjunction with thuds at our front door. It was Irene, Simon's mum, standing in the cold in just her nightdress. Ray had come home tanked up on whiskey and thrown her out into the street.

It was abhorrent, really. Irene had worked hard all day in the home, practically being chained to the kitchen sink, and it was the last thing she needed or deserved come the end of the day. She was begging Dave to help her as she wanted to get back into the house, but the door was locked, and Ray was deliberately ignoring her pleas. Dave walked her up the garden path to the entrance only to find the door had since been unlocked and was ajar. He strolled into the very unflattering sight of Ray standing in just his Y fronts, cooking sausages on the stove by shaking them persistently in the frying pan with the hot fat splashing everywhere.

As he was of a thin build, his pants were baggy although designed to be a tight fit, and the original colour of white was now an off-grey. The vision in front of him made Dave cringe as Ray wasn't the most hygienic person, so god knows how long he had been wearing those pants! Of all the states Ray got into, it amused me how his toupee always remained attached to his scalp. Dave asked him: "What the hell's going on, Ray?" He was met with an outburst of: "Fuck off, Dave. Just get out of my fucking house. Get out." Dave knew it was time to leave as Irene sneaked up to bed, and Ray would probably just pass out after his food.

Scott adored Simon, and so did I. They loved climbing trees, especially the one we had in our front garden. Many a time, I would find them both perched high up seated on the branch. Their friendship had positive effects on Simon, who seemed to gain confidence and come out of his shell. There was always a concern niggling in me about this lovely boy, but I couldn't put my finger on it. Only time would tell.

Myself and Dave on our wedding day with my mum and Dave's dad to the left. Stan and Connie to the right.

Another little boy to come on the scene was Stephen, a polite and smartly-dressed kid, a bit different from the others, who came from a hard-working, quiet family. They entered my kitchen together, and I was introduced to him by Scott. His face lit up when he smiled, this being the first thing I noticed about him which tickled me. Even though I didn't know a lot about his family, we had more in common than I thought possible. As time developed, it was bigger than I could ever imagine.

Prime Minister Maggie Thatcher's 'right to buy' scheme was the new trend circulating around the working class. Her policy of get a job, buy some shares and save for a rainy day seemed appealing to me. So, in 1987, we bit the bullet and bought our council house.

Always having been a stay-at-home mum, I thought it time to better ourselves, and I landed a part time job. The kids were getting a bit older and more manageable, and because my mum was on hand to help during school holidays, it was possible. First, I did a bit of cleaning in the evening at offices which were a 30-minute walk from the house. Later, I changed to doing bar work and waitressing on a 10 am to 2 pm shift, four days a week. It was pin money, really, which I kept for the kids if they needed any extra bits.

Dave was very equipped, having been a qualified roof tiler, and could turn his hand to most building work. He replaced our windows to double glazing and built a porch on the front of the house. He decorated it throughout and fitted a new kitchen and bathroom. He could be very useful when he put his mind to it. He had constant money-making ideas going on and with any extra cash he made, I was treated to some good-quality gold, either a fancy necklace or a bracelet.

We also had some really great family holidays at Butlins, which the kids loved and entered into all the competitions. When work was scarce, which was common in the early 1980s, Dave would get stuck into scrap dealing or buying and selling either furniture or tobacco. I remember opening the wardrobe one day and a mountain of tobacco packets fell out on top of me. I had to laugh because he always had a stash of something hidden somewhere. The bills were always paid come what may, and the kitchen cupboards were never bare, but Dave could be his own worst enemy.

Dave's father was a Polish emigrant with a surname of Dakowski who died at the age of 38 of a brain hemorrhage while in the bathroom one morning. Dave was only three years old at the time, so he never really had the chance to get to know his father. His death came totally unexpected and left the family shell-shocked. Dave's mother, Connie, was born and bred in Swindon, and when her husband died she was solely responsible to provide for their four children. She wasn't alone for very long as she met and later married an Eastender called Mitch Rosenstein, who took on the family lock, stock and barrel and was a wonderful man. He was the son of a successful Jewish tailor in

London. With his family wealth and his own painting and decorating business, Mitch and Connie were able to purchase the bungalow where I had stayed in the first year of my marriage.

They added to their brood by bearing a further four children together, plus adopting a daughter, bringing the total to nine. All the children took his surname, which he had since dropped to Rose. As Connie was a nurse, caring was in her nature, and because of her love of children she also became a foster mum, with numerous kids coming and going over the years.

There was one little boy in particular, aged twelve, who made a real impact on the family as he would run out of the house for no reason anytime of the day or night. He was sprinting to nowhere, but he would just keep going until Dave was told: "Go on Dave, go and get him"—and would chase him and bring him back home. From then on, it was Dave's job to catch the kid they nicknamed 'The Road Runner' whenever he decided to go take off. As the house was always bustling, Dave used to say that every time he came to breakfast there would be a new face staring back from the table. It was comical the way he used to tell the story, and how that woman did it, I will never know. Both Connie and Mitch were teetotallers.

One day, Mitch came home from work feeling unwell. He went to his bedroom and, after falling backwards on the bed, suffered a fatal heart attack, aged 66. Connie carried on, but years later she began showing the signs of dementia. When it became unsafe for her to stay unsupervised in her house, as she was leaving the cooker on, she was placed in a nursing home. Her family visit her often, which is one of the benefits of having lots of children.

As the kids reached their early teens, I needed some independence. So, I learnt to drive. This was against Dave's beliefs of "a woman's place is in the home," as he had grown up in an environment where the girls in the house did everything for the men. Also, perhaps, he felt he was losing control.

Driving widened my options, and I was successful in applying for a temporary admin role at a building society. It was still part-time, and the hours suited the family. I kept my nose down and worked

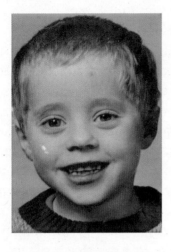

Scott aged 3   *Scott aged 8*

hard, with my efforts paying off as I was promoted to a trainer, which also paved the way to involvement in large projects and became permanent. This was the first time we were both bringing in regular money.

Although the winter periods meant Dave was rained off a lot from the site, we still had my wages, so we got by. If we never had the money, we would go without as he was good like that, not being one to get into debt. He was shrewd with the finances, and it was something

Scott and Tilly together as youngsters

I never got involved with as he took care of it. As time went by, I hated having to ask him if I wanted something like a pair of shoes, which was the reason I was keen to earn my own money. When I was younger it didn't bother me, but I had grown as a person and no longer wanted to be the 'little woman'.

CHAPTER SIX

P oor mum just wasn't herself, and it had been going on for quite a while. But we couldn't fathom what was wrong with her. The medics were also baffled by her symptoms of dropping things, short temperedness and weight loss. Finally, after many tests, the doctors diagnosed her condition to be Parkinson's disease, a brutal and unrelenting illness. Ironically, it was the same fate as Betty's, who had died four years previous of this exact condition.

It was devastating watching mum go downhill slowly and become a shadow of her former self. She had the tremors on one side of her body, which then transferred the effect to the other side of her body. She would walk with a shuffle, which is a common characteristic of Parkinson's, and she suffered a serious decline in her mobility over a six-year period.

Dad had been responsible for her care over these years, and the strain was beginning to weigh him down. So, he would admit her to hospital on occasion for a respite. It was so upsetting for us all to see her suffering, and to put it bluntly, if she had been an animal they would have put her down. I don't mean that in a disrespectful way, but it would have been the kindest course of action. I knew her, and she hated being like that, not even being able to go to the toilet unassisted.

For two years, dad had been housebound as mum needed around the clock assistance, and he wouldn't dare leave her, even for a minute. I would go shopping for him and collect her medication as the day job still needed to be done. When I was at work one day, I received a telephone call from the hospital asking me to come straight away as mum was very ill. "You must come now," they said. I thought it strange as I didn't even know she was in hospital because dad never mentioned it.

I spoke to him, and he confirmed it was the case, but he said that, because he had to go out, he would go up there later. I realised he couldn't face what maybe were the final stages of her life, as she was his life. I ran from work in the hope that I could say goodbye to her. Sadly, I got there five minutes too late. She had gone at the age 66. No age at all, really.

In her mind, she was aware the end was near and would say: "Will you pray for me, Julie?" My response was: "Of course I will mum. I promise."

I still wanted to see her one last time, so the staff let me in, only to find her soul and warmth had already drifted away. She had been such a vibrant and energetic lady, and there she was, lying so tiny and weak. But I knew she was at peace and in a better place. She always thought that you go on somewhere else as her saying was "death is not the end." I was 34 years old and felt too young to have lost her. I expected her to live until old age, so believed I was robbed of a further 20 years of having a mother.

After that, everywhere I went I kept seeing her. But, of course, it wasn't mum, just someone who looked like her. I kept my promise, and even now I will go to the Catholic Church to light a candle as she loved doing that, like she did in the convent all those years ago.

My dear mum. Not a great start in life and a sad ending, but the bit in the middle was great for her and that's what's important. For the next six months after her death, dad started drinking at home. So, whenever I went around to the house he was flying at 50,000 feet on vodka, not a drink he would normally consume, and he let things slide. Luckily, he didn't go down a slippery slope for too long as he came to his senses and came to the conclusion life goes on, and he must go on with it. I commend the way he picked himself up, which showed he had strength of character.

We got on with our lives as you don't have much option, really, and I turned my full focus on the kids. Scott was turning into a lovely young man. He had a lovely nature, and we had a strong bond. We could talk about anything to each other and could even read each other's minds. He would say: "I know what you're thinking mum."

"Oh yeah, what?" would be my reaction. He would go on to explain: "I know what you're thinking. We have the same minds me and you." And he was right. It's that intuitive thing. I was pleased he had remained strong friends with Stephen as they had similar personalities and were good for one another. He got involved in karate and fishing when he was young and even became a ball boy for Swindon Town Football Club.

Our philosophy as parents was to get them involved in different activities to stimulate their minds. Tilly took up ballet and Irish dancing, even winning trophies as she became so good. Academically at school, she was a high achiever but never really knew what she wanted to do. For Scott, however, there was no choice; he was adamant that carpentry was the only career for him.

He was always good at making things. I would watch him dismantle toys and then put them back together again, even from the tender age of three. Upon finishing school, he enrolled at the local college for a three-year carpentry course. By the end of the training, he was flying high, achieving levels 1 and 2 of City and Guilds qualifications in joinery and carpentry, and I couldn't have been more proud of him.

He started working on site quite soon after becoming qualified, and he began mixing with other tradesmen. As a junior carpenter, he was responsible for putting up stud walls, so he needed some tools, but mainly a nail gun in order to do the job, which cost me £500. He was over the moon with it and got to work straight away on a project of newly built houses, right beside one of the town's two colleges and on the bus route into the centre.

Swindon was expanding faster than ever, which led to a shortage in accommodation. The majority were two-beds and were relatively small in size, but they were government-funded for people on the housing association scheme.

The world was Scott's oyster and was opening up for him in many ways. At times he worked alongside his dad, but they didn't always see eye to eye as Dave had his way of doing things and Scott his. As he was trained by college, Scott did things by the book, but Dave learnt by what he saw, so the differences in their personalities were plain to see. The word compromise didn't come into Dave's vocabulary, so it would lead to a clash. In fact, Dave's stubborn attitude was becoming progressively worse, not just at work but in the home too.

He was volatile, more so than in the past, and it did our marriage no favours as the arguments at times escalated and became more frequent between us. Things were going downhill, but we didn't know it was creeping up on us. His behaviour caused friction in the household, upsetting Scott and Tilly. He was earning the best money he ever had, so you would have expected for life to have got better, but that wasn't the case.

Having more disposable cash gave Dave the freedom to go out drinking with his mates, both after work and on a Saturday night. However, Saturday night became increasingly earlier, and he would start the session at one o'clock in the afternoon. He must have made a reputation for himself at the local pub as he was forever moaning about 'some fucking arsehole' or another. I used to think the one common denominator in all these arguments was Dave himself.

When he finally stumbled home, he would be verbally abusive towards me for no reason, so I started to ensure I was already in bed to deter anything flaring up. That didn't stop him as one night he just barged in almost like he had made it his mission to hunt me down the minute he arrived home. I was fast asleep only to be awoken by the quilt cover being yanked off disturbing the warmth of my body and to a barrage of: "You did this and you did that." I tried to keep calm and not engage in a row with him. Totally unprovoked, he flung the wardrobe door open and proceeded to throw my clothes out of the window. I didn't know what the hell he was playing at. The next thing he was standing in the garden throwing tomato ketchup all over my belongings. I thought it was strange as commonly a person would set them a light not squeeze sauce on them. What's he going to do? Eat them?!

I saw red and marched to the kitchen, only he wouldn't let up and followed me, allowing me no space. Then a scuffle took place, and he slapped me around the head. Trying to dodge him, I stumbled backwards and fell onto the hard, granite tiles, which hurt my legs. So, I reached for the nearest object in retaliation. What I had grabbed hold of was a small frying pan, the sort used for omelettes. It was still warm underneath. Tilly had not long been home after a night out partying with the girls and had cooked eggs before going to bed flat out of it.

At full force, I smashed it into his face and, due to the heat and speed at which it made contact, it stuck and was just hanging. I don't agree with violence, and I was actually shocked at myself, but I think I snapped after enduring his verbal aggression over a prolonged period. That little episode landed Dave in A&E as his skin was badly burned, but he was discharged hours later once the diagonal scorch mark under his nose leading down to his lip was assessed.

When he did arrive home, Dave was full of defiance and thought I should be grateful that he only said 'my wife' did it to me without divulging my identity, to prevent me from getting into trouble. He seemed proud of himself that he had the nouse to give himself the false name of John James, and of being able to do so off the top of his head while in shock.

I never understood his behaviour and often felt that I had done something wrong, but the truth was I hadn't. The problem lay with him and the way in which he handled his feelings. It was hard to get him to open up, and communication is key to a relationship. He had to have his own way, and if he didn't get it then he would act like a spoiled brat. I found this baffling as he came from a large family, and his mother wouldn't have had time to spoil him. I was so curious that I once asked Connie where this all came from. She enlightened me that Dave's grandfather had spoiled him rotten as a youngster, which had done him no favours, but finally I had found the missing piece of the jigsaw.

CHAPTER SEVEN

Tilly was content enough and found herself a job in an office for the local council. She was doing well and had her own circle of friends. She had always been a private person. She wouldn't let you in easily, and only then until she felt comfortable with you. To get on with things quietly was her nature, but she did have her moments if rubbed up the wrong way.

Scott's attitude, however, started to change, and I couldn't understand why. Most blatant was his lying in bed in the morning rather than getting up for work. He had been so conscientious before to make a good impression and look smart, always making sure that thick, wavy hair looked right and tamed. But now it was left to run wild. He had also started smoking, which we as a family hated, as none of us smoked. And to top it off, he admitted it wasn't just cigarettes, but weed as well. This disappointed me as he seemed to be making wrong decisions, choices I would never have associated him with. I tried to talk him out of smoking all together, and he said: "I will. I won't keep doing it. I will pack up soon."

Trying to look for reasons and answers, I thought perhaps he'd had too much, too soon as he was earning £800 on average per week, as I used to bank his cheques. This was a colossal amount of money for a 19-year-old living at home, not just in 1998, but even today, and it wasn't lasting. He kept running out before his next pay cheque, so he would ask me to sub him, which I did. He did always pay me back, along with the £500 I coughed up for the nail gun, but as it got worse, Dave lost his patience and kept having a go at him.

I thought that, as Scott had been going out a lot with his mates, and because he had a new girlfriend, this is where his money must be going. Emily had recently come onto the scene, and they were smitten with one another, and well-suited. She was beautiful, with long, flowing blonde hair all the way down her back, which was her most striking feature. They had met at a nightclub as she was visiting her mum in Swindon at her five-bedroom detached house, but Emily usually lived in Wales with her father.

Scott treated her and other girls really well, and I think it's because he had such a good relationship with me, his mum, that it transferred over to other females. On occasion he would express to me his disapproval of the way in which his dad would speak to me as he thought it disrespectful.

I persisted with my questioning as in my head I couldn't lay it to rest. So, Scott admitted that the older workers on site had offered him blow, which he accepted. It never clicked with me as I knew no one who took blow or any kind of drugs. My knowledge on the subject was pretty much zero. This went on for a while as I struggled to understand why he would need to smoke it, and it ended up in a row. Dave didn't really grasp the seriousness of it as he was either too busy working or socialising with his mates.

A few weeks later, Scott lost his job as the foreman fired him. He told me that the work had run out, but I knew that wasn't true. The real reason was that his colleagues had been complaining about his lack of concentration and motivation. He worked in a dangerous environment with heavy duty tools and had become a liability. Plus his attendance was poor, and he couldn't be relied upon to turn up.

Not long after, I kept finding tin foil in his bedroom. But not knowing what it was for, I dismissed it as unimportant. He continued to lounge on his bed and listen to music, his favourite being Oasis or The Verve. He loved that sound, only now it was without any energy in his being. Oddly enough, I didn't realise how connected he was to the song 'The Drugs Don't Work' because I was unaware at the time. But the lyrics summed it up. Then one day, Tilly screamed out: "Mum quick, come here now!" I ran upstairs to find her standing in his bedroom shaking.

"Look at this," she said and pointed down to a hypodermic needle lying next to her feet. I looked down at this small but deadly object and was in complete shock. My mind suddenly reverted back to similar feelings I had when I got lost on the beach as a child, that live or die situation, I guess. I knew I had to have tenacity to deal with this, but I was very unaware of just how much at this point. I felt fearful and sick in that all the good things I had left in my life were being sucked away.

He was using HEROIN, not just smoking it, I realized as the reason for the tin foil suddenly came to light, but also injecting it!! I was beside myself, when I thought he was just dabbling in blow. But this, this is something else! I knew in my mind this was massive and didn't know what to do. Then I had this flood of panic and confusion run over me like a tsunami. How do I approach this? Do I completely lose it or stay calm and try to reason with him? All these emotions ravaged through me, whilst still trying to comprehend why he would make such a terrible choice in his life.

Scott came back to the house from wherever he had been, probably from getting drugs, so I sat him down and asked him straight out. It didn't help matters that Tilly was shouting and screaming in the background calling him all sorts, but only because she worried about him so much. With the intention of not going off my head, I said rationally: "Scott, why are you doing this to yourself? It's so dangerous. Why would you use heroin, WHY? He explained that his mates were all into it, so he thought he would try it. From that I took it that peer pressure had lead him down this path, and the only thing I knew at this time was you just have to get off it or it will take over your life, so how do I get him clean?

I braced myself to tell Dave when he got home. I was dreading it, but it had to be done. When I disclosed the bombshell, he just lost it and chucked Scott out of the house. Dave didn't lay a finger on him but was shouting and balling and squared up to Scott eyeball to eyeball, so Scott knew it was best to get out of his way. As Dave and I hadn't been getting on anyway, this was the cherry on the cake, although I hoped it could possibly unite us but it had the opposite effect.

Scott went to my dad's for a while as I thought if anyone can sort him out, Stanley can. I couldn't bring myself to tell dad the real reason behind the falling out. I didn't want him knowing, to prevent myself feeling shame and to avoid unwanted questions. I wasn't ready to explain to anyone, even dad, as I still hadn't absorbed the news myself. I made out that Scott and Dave had an argument over general issues. I did not reveal the full extent of his drug problem, although dad did have an idea some kind of drug was involved. It was unfair, really, but I thought keeping him in the dark was probably the best option for now as I expected to resolve Scott's problem fairly quickly.

Things were going well for a while, but then dad complained that Scott was acting strange, and that all the tablespoons were going missing from the drawer. I knew straight away what that meant: He was using again. Heroin is placed on a spoon, then over a lighted flame, mixed with citric acid or lemon juice in order to burn it down. A filter is then placed on the spoon to take out any impurities from the liquid formula before the syringe draws it up. Then you have it; you've got your fix. Dad also couldn't get his head around the fact that Scott had no shoe laces in his trainers at times. He was obviously using the laces to tie off injection sites, but you would never see any track marks as he constantly wore long sleeves, even in the warmer weather, but I knew they must be there.

A gang of lads were constantly coming to the house. They would firstly stand in the hallway, whispering to one another, then suddenly trail upstairs, along with Scott. One time Stanley got so fed up with it, referring to them as 'his cocky mates', and was at a loss as to what they were up to. So, he followed them up unexpectedly. He barged into the bedroom and told them all to get out quite firmly whilst making a movement with his thumb, the same as a hitch-hiker would do.

Another thing that used to annoy Stanley is that Scott wasn't interested in sitting with him in the evening to enjoy watching a film together. After all, Scott was his guest, and Stanley had welcomed him into his home. Instead, it was more like living with a 'jack in the box' that couldn't sit still for a minute. Scott would leave the house without a moment's notice and come back at all hours, so Stanley was unsure whether he was safe to go bed or should wait up.

Food was in the cupboard, but it was down to Scott to cook his own meals as my dad wasn't prepared to pamper him. Luckily, Scott was pretty domesticated and could cook, as he had watched me many a time since he was small and had taken an interest. He and dad were never particularly close, but they did have regular contact throughout his life, so there was a kind of bond. But Scott wouldn't get too deep in a conversation with him. After a few months, Scott had left a pan on the hob. The pan burnt to a cinder and could have set the house alight, so Stanley finally lost patience. He couldn't cope with Scott anymore and sent him back home to me.

I hadn't seen very much of Scott whilst he was staying with my dad. It took the pressure off my own household for a while, but Scott consumed my thoughts as I was continuously worrying about what he was getting up to. Stanley had been living in a situation with a blindfold, as he didn't know Scott had a serious addiction. This was all alien to him. Drugs just weren't part of dad's era. He was used to seeing someone needing a skinful but not this! However, once I told him the truth, to my surprise he was sympathetic and said he had taken notice of what drugs had done to even talented people in the limelight, so he could understand how serious this was. I was just thankful my mum was not around to witness the drug scene as it would have been so worrisome for her. I have no doubt she would have done anything to help as she was a compassionate person.

CHAPTER EIGHT

Scott's behaviour in general deteriorated, having no interest in anything apart from drugs and listening to music. Even his relationship with his devoted girlfriend, Emily, started to fail. He was treating her quite badly by stitching her up on arranged meetings or not calling when he said he would. He would even leave her sitting in his bedroom for hours as he would suddenly get up and clear out. I was aware she was sitting there all alone, so I did offer for her to come down and have a chat, but she politely refused and said she was fine to wait. The lovingness from him had diminished, which was totally out of character, and it caused her to turn up on my doorstep in floods of tears.

She was unaware when she first began dating him that he was on drugs. Later, when the truth emerged, she still only thought he was smoking the stuff, not that he was injecting. Although I thought she was the ideal person for my son, I had to inform her how big the problem was. Therefore, in so many words, I said: "Emily, it's best you walk away, at least for now." I couldn't sit back and watch him treat her like that. She didn't deserve it, and perhaps this was the short sharp shock he needed to come to his senses.

Reflecting back, I never envisaged drugs would come into my family. So, I really didn't know how we had come to this. Everything in my world felt wrong, not normal anymore, and no matter how I tried to get things back on track, it never worked. The knock-on effect was catastrophe as the relationship between me and Tilly came to boiling point several times over Scott's lifestyle.

It was disrupting everyday life as it appeared I was favouring him over her because I worried about him so much. I always put him first and forgot about how Tilly was feeling, but it was only because I wanted to save him so desperately. I saw the potential in him as a young man, which made it harder to take. Such a talented boy, but it was all wasting away before my eyes. You are helpless as long as you have that poison in your life as nothing will ever be the same. If you try it once or twice you may escape its hold, but the more times you use, it will certainly take you down the road to destruction, no question.

I could not fight this alone. He needed some kind of medical help. By admitting this, I was starting to feel that drug addiction is more powerful than us, contrary to my own belief that the human mind can overcome anything. After visiting the doctors, Scott was referred to a clinic in the town centre called Druglink. They do not offer counselling, but instead, place the user on a methadone script. This is a heroin substitute which is used to wean you off the drug, although it can be addictive in itself. This, however, is only dealing with the physical symptoms whilst the mental symptoms are neglected.

Methadone liquid is taken orally behind the counter at the pharmacy, supervised by a member of staff. The dosage is regularly reviewed with the assumption your body needs less over time, to eventually become substance-free.

Where drug addicts are concerned, there would always be a scam as they become intelligent in their drive to score. I was discovering more about what happens on the street and becoming accustomed to this drug-street talk, as once money and drugs have exchanged hands the user has 'scored'.

Methadone was sold on the black market and abused, as then both substances are used side by side to get a bigger hit at a lower price. There is some respite whilst they are on the prescription, but there is always a worry they are using both. To remain on a methadone programme, the requirement is to participate in mandatory drug tests via urine samples. This is to prove you are not using drugs as well, and if tested positive, your prescription would automatically stop. Again, the addicts would cheat the system by using a drug-free person's urine already peed in a tube and passed off as their own.

Druglink soon got wind of this, and toilet visits then had to be held under strict supervision.

The methadone was holding Scott for a while, but as warned not to, he began using it as well as heroin. As he had lapsed, in desperation he was back on the streets trying to score. He would be out of the house for ages, and I would drive around the estate relentlessly trying to track him down. I thought that if he couldn't get out, he couldn't use. So, I tried locking him in his bedroom. I didn't force this upon him; he chose to try this method, which worked for a brief time with me taking his food up to him and allowing him out for showers and toilet.

Scott was detoxing until the last few days, when he was shaking and sweating. He started banging on the door to be let out as he couldn't bear it anymore. I persevered and would not give in, reassuring him it was working and would soon be over. It became very tense, and I was close to breaking point after hearing him in such desperation. Suddenly, it went quiet, and I assumed he had fallen asleep. But, no, he had taken the windowpane out of the frame then jumped from the top floor in his search for drugs.

This was the start of another cycle, which resulted in him stealing money and anything in the house that he could get his hands on: gold, watches, CDs, and even clothes. You name it, and he would take it. Those types of things wouldn't be around for long as they were easy to sell on. Even his once-cherished nail gun got flogged. Items were constantly going missing. He even drew money from my credit card; how he managed that I do not know to this day. By this point, I had stopped giving him money as it was obvious what it was for. I tried to claw back some control, so if he needed clothes, I would buy them for him or take him shopping.

The trouble is, once they have the clothes, they can either sell them for money or trade them for drugs, so you never eradicate the vicious circle. He even pawned the guitar I bought him, the one thing he promised he would never do, which saddened me deeply as it meant he had given away part of himself. Scott had shown an interest in music, so I purchased him the instrument in the hope he would get a different kind of pleasure, a deflection from drugs. The guilt about selling this particular item, which he so badly wanted, rose up within him, and he confessed to me what he had done.

I ended up buying it back from the pawn shop, meaning I had paid twice for it, but I didn't care. It was symbolic. When he pulled himself together, which he managed to do for brief periods, Scott would do cash-in-hand carpentry jobs. However, this just meant he had more money to buy drugs when he weakened.

One day, he got up and was withdrawing badly and in desperate need of a fix. As the drugs were wearing out of his system, the flu-like symptoms were kicking in, which is dubbed 'clucking', from the term 'cold turkey'. Scott had abdominal cramps and the shakes, which would last approximately four days if he didn't refill his system with more drugs. Even if he had got past this period, his physical dependency would have ceased, but his mind would still have been telling him he needed more. He was so weak and ill, not feeling strong enough to go out and score himself, so begged me to take him to a known supplier. He only asked me to do this once, in desperation, and when you see your child in that state, it drives you crazy. I would never have considered doing something so seedy before, but I was in a different world now and played by different rules.

We got in the car, and he directed me to where we needed to go, but not to a council estate. Oh no, we are talking middle-class suburbia. We pulled up to a neat and tidy semi, and the person who answered the door wasn't some big-time dealer in gold chains with a flashy car on the drive. It was an ordinary member of the public, not distinguishable in any way, and it shocked me. I felt really uncomfortable and knew I didn't want to be part of this; it was a life of forever looking over your shoulder. I made it very clear to Scott that I wouldn't be doing this again, and he sat silently during the ride home.

Because of his addiction, I began to know of many different types of people who sell drugs, and I mean class A. There was even an old-age pensioner who would pull up in his Ford Fiesta and drop the drugs off at the front door. Had my mind not been so chaotic, I would have taken down the number plate and shopped it to the Drug

Squad. I was so angry and wanted to fight back at this somehow in my own way.

I was forever in Scott's bedroom scouring around for clues as to where he was, but I knew we weren't any further forward as the usual chestnut of burnt silver foil, plastic wraps and used needles were present.

It was driving me insane. My brain was consumed with it, and I was unable to give my focus to anything else, including work. In the depths of his addiction, Scott's behaviour was becoming more and more erratic: One minute he was drowsy and the next all hyper. I was at a loss as to why and what else was affecting him.

The heroin tends to make the users chilled out and sleepy, and it gives them a droopy appearance as the effect on the body makes it feel heavy. Their pupils are like little pin holes, a major sign to look out for. They are also unaware of their surroundings, but here he was, racing around at full speed, so I knew something was different. He was cleaning his bedroom, washing his clothes and bathing more than usual, but it's normally the opposite. He became quick to react if you challenged him, which again was out of character as he wasn't a confrontational person. Then an explanation to all of this surfaced when I discovered a pipe-type object covered in tin foil under his bed. I picked it up and kept looking at it inquisitively, wondering what the hell it was.

There was a small hole in the foil that sat across the top opening of the tube, so I knew quite quickly it was an object used for inhaling. Through the grapevine, I had heard that crack use was exploding throughout the town, but I never took any notice of it. I was dealing with heroin, not crack! Then the penny started to drop. This was the reason for the change in him. He was also using crack—could this situation get any worse? They can also burn crack in things like asthma inhalers and coke cans punctured with small holes which then enable them to inhale the vapour. It is called crack because of the crackling sound it makes when burnt, giving the user a quick 'rush'.

I collared him about my findings, but of course he denied it. Lying was part of his personality now, but we both knew the truth.

From then on, this is how it continued: heroin, crack, heroin and so forth. The typical £10-a-day heroin habit now increased to £20 as Scott was buying the two substances in one hit. The more he used, the more his body needed to feel satisfied as his tolerance levels increased. So, his daily bill had now reached £40 (£20 for the heroin and £20 for the crack).

The reason for taking the two in conjunction with each other is because heroin takes them down, and then the crack is used to bring them back up. Crack is a nasty drug causing the user to become psychotic and schizophrenic if taken over time. Speedballs are another common practice, which is where the heroin and crack are injected together. The interactions of using both drugs are not fully understood within the clinical profession. So, the outcomes for these types of users are still not known. Ripped packets of citric acid were another regular fixture strewn across his room, along with small pieces of plastic used to wrap the drugs in.

CHAPTER NINE

One Friday when I finished work early, I came into the house only to observe Dave's cricket set being carried out by Scott's friend, Rodney. Rodney was a cocky red-head with matching coloured freckles sprinkled all over his face. His hair colour defined his fiery personality as he had one hell of a temper and had inherited his mother's sarcasm.

He had been a visitor to our house since the age of five and had now grown to six feet tall with a slim build. When he rubbed me up the wrong way, I bit my lip and took into consideration his traumatic childhood and didn't retaliate. Rodney's father walked out when he was two years old, and they boy lived with just his mum until she took up with a new partner and had a second child. He then found himself with a new stepdad and half-brother, but it wasn't a happy home for Rodney. The stepfather was cruel to him and treated him very differently from his own child. He would slap Rodney around and wake him up in the middle of the night to take a cold shower, all happening when Rodney's mum was out. Rodney was too scared to tell her. So, his anger festered, which made him the way he was. However, years later, when she did find out, she kicked him out of the house.

The two lads were together, so I knew instantly they were up to no good and that it involved drugs. So, they probably were looking for something to sell. I said: "What the hell do you think you are doing, Rodney?" Dave was away working, which was a damn good job as he would have blown his top had he seen this. With that, Rodney just jumped in his car with the bats and roared off, and my gut reaction was to follow him.

The adrenaline was flowing around my body as I drove through the streets of Swindon. It was like a scene from one of those police chase movies, and I was totally out of my depth. I tailed him all the way until I managed to corner him down a one-way street. Yes, checkmate, I had him! He slammed on his brakes and got out of the car in the middle of the road. His anger was plain to see as I emerged from my vehicle.

He opened the boot of his car and pulled out one of the cricket bats, getting in position to take a swing at me. I was petrified but didn't show it. I kept my nerve and said: "Rodney just give me the cricket set. If Dave finds out, make no mistake, he will kill you. But if you do the right thing, he doesn't need to know." The truth is that Dave would never go so far as to inflict physical violence. He was more about making a noise. I was trying to put the fear of god into Rodney, but it didn't seem to be working as he replied: "Stay back or you will get this over your head." I had to call his bluff and bring this stand-off to an end, as we were in full view of passers-by.

"Go on then. If you think you're such a big man, go for it if you feel the need to have a pop at a woman. You don't have it in you, Rodney. I know it's the drugs making you do this, the crack and the heroin. I know the score. I am Scott's mum, so my eyes are open to it. I have known you since you were a little boy. What's happened to you? Come on, Rodney. This is all wrong, and you know it."

My spiel must have hit a raw nerve as he began to break down and slump towards the floor whilst sobbing: "You don't understand what it's like. It's hell, plain and simple."

I told him to get some help and stop this crazy lifestyle before it's too late. I then reclaimed the cricket set and made my way home. My head was racing with scenes from the day, but in all honesty, days like this were becoming too normal for me. Only this wasn't normal. Far from it. But it would be part of my life until I found some cure for my son. It was all so heartbreaking, and I thought I was in some kind of nightmare which would all end soon, and I would just wake up.

I tried to tackle the problem from a different angle and went in with the 'tough love' approach. I told Scott to pack his things and leave, but he refused to go. So, I waited until he went out and then wouldn't let him back in when he returned. He sat outside for ages, begging me to open the door. "Mum, let me in. Let me in, mum! Let me in." My heart was yearning, so I had to put my hands over my ears to block out his voice.

Tilly was adamant, and I probably would have cracked if it wasn't for her saying: 'Don't let him back in here; you have to teach him a lesson.' I knew I had to stand my ground, but my worry was that he would clear off and be found out of it in some crack den. As the hours went on, and he was still sitting there with the temperature getting colder, I succumbed and let him back in for his own welfare. By his own request, I locked him in his room several times to go cold turkey, even though he had failed at this before. You have to be tenacious. Old habits die hard, and again he would manage to unpick the lock on the window or feed me a sob story to get out. As soon as my back was turned, he would be sneaking out to score. He was very crafty, and that stuff was reaching parts of his brain only other addicts would understand.

Whenever a quiet moment would arise, which wasn't very often in our home anymore, I would reflect and ask how my boy Scott could be hooked on heroin at age 19. How did I miss that? Was it down to me and Dave, something we did or didn't do?

He was such a happy little boy growing up, who never caused us any problems, and Tilly never touched drugs or smoked. I could reach no answers, yet I found myself dissecting my life piece by piece for how this came about. You feel a strong sense of disappointment, but you love them no matter what as they are your children, so your feelings are unconditional.

I didn't care what people thought. I was going through hell. This is the hand I had been dealt, and I would have to play it to the best of my ability. I would look around at other parents with grown-up children and think: "Why are they so normal?" Everyone else seemed to be living the dream with their offspring either going off to university or thriving in their chosen careers. What have they done that I haven't? I would stare and watch them from the side-lines, appearing to be trouble-free.

Well that is how it seemed from the outside looking in, and again would say: "Why me?" Unless you have gone through such an experience, it's hard to understand. It's a subject that is swept under the carpet, and unless it's your son or daughter, who really wants to know about drugs and that ugly world?

Only after being in this nightmare do I know what addiction is, as I was living the life of an addict without actually using the drugs. This would be the same scenario for any kind of substance abuse, including the main one that is socially accepted, alcohol, and the biggest killer, cigarettes.

Manipulating the drug world from the other end of the spectrum were two brothers I had known since they were knee-high, and pushed about in a pram. They weren't even acquaintances, just a family I would see around our area as I was going about my business. They were born to a single mother, Kirsty, who had five children in total, all from different fathers.

Kirsty had four boys in a row who were all mixed-race. She herself was white, but each of her partners was black. Her fifth child was white, her first and only girl, and she would struggle with her multitude of tots doubled up in the pushchair. Kirsty was only about 18 when she had her first baby, Dwight. She was a very slim and pretty girl with long dark hair, but as the years passed, she lost her attractiveness and looked tired. Dwight, who had a lovely nature, got sucked into the drug scene. He tried for years to get clean, even going to rehab a few times and moved away to another town. He abstained for periods but was always drawn back into that world. His two younger brothers, however, Tyrone and Cain, were big-time dealers. They never touched the stuff themselves; they weren't stupid. They used to have runners, who are addicts that sell the gear for the dealers in return for being supplied with drugs as payment.

Tyrone and Cain would go out of town and buy all kinds of drugs, including pills, cocaine and anything else that would make them a profit. They never did an honest day's work in their lives but would swan around in the best cars and wear the latest designer clothes, along with solid-gold jewellery hanging from their necks and wrists. They were both in their mid-twenties, short and slim and relatively good-looking. They later opened shops to launder all the cash they were making, but it was just a front to hide their dirty money. I think these types of people are the worst kind as they are not using themselves but living off the back of the misery drugs cause. To me they are like mass-murderers, destroying families with no conscience.

I found out that Scott was doing some carpentry work for them, and I hit the roof as it was obvious they would pay him with drugs. Every morning, they would call and ask him to go round to their flat, but I soon put a stop to it as I grabbed the phone off Scott whilst he was chatting to them and said: "I will get you caught one day." Cain even turned up at my door asking for Scott, but as I answered it, it gave me the opportunity to give him a piece of my mind as I screamed: "If you ever come round here again, you will be crawling down that path because you won't be able to walk." He just glared at me with an arrogant 'I don't care' look. But as they weren't violent people, they were wimps, really. I didn't feel threatened.

The brothers qualified for a local authority flat. In the eyes of the council, they were still living with their mum, had no money and were not earning, as all their capital was hidden. It was also a case of abusing the welfare system as they were eligible for dole money so would sign on each fortnight without being pressured into finding work. Benefits were more of a lifestyle choice during this time as the restrictions and conditions imposed today to prove you are not work-shy did not exist so much.

Tyrone and Cain used their flat to do a lot of dealing, until one day the Drug Squad busted in and found heroin inside a shoe box that was at the back of the wardrobe. The Old Bill had got a tip-off at last and managed to catch them red-handed in possession of the gear. For some reason, only Tyrone, the older of the two, went to prison and was going to be banged up for seven years. Perhaps the lengthy sentence incorporated previous convictions. As for Cain, he got off due to lack of evidence, which is the whole problem the police have with catching this trash. They know they are doing it, but proving it is another matter.

Heroin seemed to be getting worse in the area, and Scott's friend Danny, who lived in a street nearby, was another youngster to be embroiled in this drug scene. Rather than shoplift to fund his habit, in desperation he created a more deceitful plan to con money out of the public. He would go up to people at random in tears and say: "Please can you help me. My stepfather beats me, and I need to get away. Can you lend me £10 or £20, so I can catch the train down to Weymouth?" His acting was worthy of an Oscar, and his boyish looks of jet-black hair, which was combed and gelled forward, the huge puppy-dog eyes and small frame certainly cracked it for him. He was onto a winner, but you couldn't help but warm to him.

Of course, there was no violent stepfather. He was a myth. But most of the time, Danny's sob story worked. He even led the unsuspecting Good Samaritan to the cash point machine and watched them withdraw the money. His antics were well-known around the town, but hundreds of people still fell for it hook, line and sinker as he was a charmer, and he even ended up in court several times.

The newspaper labelled him 'The Crying Boy', and his face was on the front page to fore-warn would-be-victims. After years of playing the abused son, it eventually wore a bit thin. Even my dad said to him one day: "Come on, Danny. You have exhausted this one to death. You need to move on to the next town." Danny followed his advice literally, which was intended as a joke, and took his business elsewhere as he was banned from most places in Swindon. However, during the height of his addiction he still managed to produce five children, so something was working right!

Danny had been through the judicial process several times when eventually they ordered him to rehabilitate at a residential drug treatment centre. As the sentence was imposed through the courts, it is funded by the system, but it is very costly if paying privately. Danny first embraced the opportunity, but after a short stay, he escaped when the coast was clear, returning to his usual ways. This is typical of someone with an addiction as they relapse several times and are very hard to treat because part of that recovery is to gain new life skills and even change the environment they live in. The demon was on Danny's back again, but like Danny, many others struggle with that psychological demon every day.

CHAPTER TEN

Tilly was slowing turning into a very highly-strung young lady as the upset and stress Scott's habit was causing was beginning to have a serious effect on her. She would constantly lose her temper and shout and scream at him: "Why can't you just stop?" Her frustrations had no effect on him; they just fell on deaf ears. I was torn between my two children, who used to be so close, in trying to help him but also attempting to protect her. The family atmosphere was dreadful. So, to balance things out, I would secretly replace any item that went missing and smooth over every argument or fight that erupted. The one thing she would say that would hit a nerve and cut deep was when she would call him a 'druggie'. He hated being labelled that and would defend himself by saying: "I'm not a druggie." Even though quite clearly he was using drugs, he hated that label as he knew he had so much more to offer.

I had to find a way through this somehow as Dave just seemed to wash his hands of the whole drug thing because he didn't know how to cope with it. He was keeping busy making money, and nothing would get in the way of that; perhaps he had his own obsession. He never had it easy and always strived to better himself. He grabbed the opportunity to join a lottery syndicate, whereas I couldn't even contemplate anything additional than the norm. Dave was jammy, and after 18 months of playing, the group won a few grand between the five of them, but it wasn't so lucky for one fellow who pulled out just before they hit the jackpot. Most of the time Dave and Scott wouldn't engage, but when Scott went out on an errand for him and didn't return for hours, it irritated Dave and he would let rip.

Dave would be quite intimidating in his manner when saying: "Where the hell have you been?" But Scott was not intimidated and stood up for himself. The pressure it put on our already rocky marriage was immense and, because he disagreed with my methods in handling the situation, it paved the way for further rows.

Dave's notion was to do 'tough love', but my fear of something happening to Scott because I had thrown him out was too great, and the guilt would have eaten away at me. No one saw Scott like I did, and I knew he was too far gone for 'tough love' as any logical sense to pull himself together had left him. Dave and I broke up at this stage due to the masses of negativity around us, and I asked him to leave, which he rejected. We had grown apart; he was living the life of a single man yet enjoying the home comforts of a married one, and merely treated the house like a hotel when he wasn't out with his mates. He wasn't supportive at all, although I couldn't lay all the blame at his feet as it's a hard thing to swallow that your only son is a heroin addict, especially when you feel you have done everything to bring him up well.

Despite Dave always letting his mouth run away with him, when it came to defending Scott from drugs or dealers he remained silent. I think we women are more equipped to cope with something as ongoing and dysfunctional as addiction. He didn't want to get involved in that world and thought it was a case of "just get off it and get on with your life." Denial is a big factor in drug addiction for the addict and the people close to them. I know that underneath, Dave was truly upset about our son being on drugs, but he didn't know how to handle it. So, ignorance was bliss. I bought Dave out of the property, giving him half the equity with which he bought a rundown place to renovate, later selling it on for a profit.

We had to live together not really getting on for ten months, which is a long time, whilst he was waiting for his new place to become liveable. I think he secretly was still holding on to the marriage, hoping it would turn out differently, but nothing seemed to be working. Even though I was now divorced, and he wasn't around anymore on a day-to-day basis, it wasn't any harder for me as I was used to coping on my own.

I wasn't completely alone in this epidemic as quite a few of the familiar young guys, including Simon and Stephen, were also hooked on heroin. Their mothers, therefore, were also fighting this disease. I noticed a change in Simon when I bumped into him in the street, which immediately took me aback. He was very gaunt and grey-looking, and although he acknowledged me with a lift of the head, he didn't stop to talk, reflecting his solemn mood.

Shortly after, another shock came when Stephen knocked at the door and entered, looking thinner and constantly scratching his arms. Scratching is a predominant sign that someone is using heroin as, when the drug is injected, it causes the body to release histamine. I then felt justified in asking if he was OK with the implication he had a habit. I tried to question him sensitively, and began with admitting Scott's problem, so as not to make him feel being picked on.

"Look," I said. "Scott is on heroin, and I get the impression you are too as you don't look your usual self."

He denied it saying: "No, no I am ok, really. There is no way I would touch that stuff."

I continued, as I cared and because I could see the same destruction in him as I did my own son. "Stephen, I'm not stupid I can tell the signs, so be honest with me."

With that he went quiet before murmuring: "Well, OK, you're right. But I am getting treatment, so will get off it for good."

I finished my conversation firmly, saying: "Make sure that you do, please, for your own sake and your mum's." So, there it was. The three S's: Scott, Simon and Stephen, all tied up in this addiction. Where did it come from? Who introduced it to them? How much worse could it get? Well, it could get worse. Even my friend Gina's daughter, Faye, who was once a delightful child brought up solely by her mother, was now totally in its clutches. She was the first female I knew to be using as prior to this it had been all males.

Faye was the person who was using the pensioner to deliver the gear to her door, and the consequences were on another level as it was the worst case of heroin addiction I have ever seen! She was a pretty girl, with medium-length dark hair, who started out with the right intentions. After finishing school, she got a job working in an office and was doing well until she fell in with a bad crowd. The cost of her daily drugs was so high that shoplifting could no longer cover it. So, she was selling her body in the red-light district. As her income grew, so did her habit, as she was making big money raking in hundreds of pounds every night for both her and her pimp. Some clients would turn nasty after having their wicked way and would just kick her out in the middle of nowhere like a piece of trash, without paying. She attended court on a regular basis.

Nothing seemed to shock Faye into getting clean, even after being badly injured in a car crash that was caused by her drug-addicted boy-friend. When in hospital to be treated for her injuries, which included a fractured spine and a badly broken nose, she was withdrawing and made a full spectacle of herself, shouting and screaming "fuck off and get me some drugs" to the nurses when they were assisting her wounds. Her mum invited me to her house in desperation for support over her daughter's addiction and wanted to show me the awful truth.

She took me upstairs to see Faye's bedroom. Upon opening the door, I felt like I was looking at a scene from *The Texas Chainsaw Massacre* movie. It took my breath away as there were mounds of blood splattered and sprayed everywhere, up the walls, on the floor, even on the ceiling, from where she had been injecting. Gina would redecorate the bedroom with a new lick of paint every so often, only for it to be bloodied again within a few weeks.

It was then that it really hit home as to what this drug can do to a person, and I can't think of anything else in the drug world that cuts into you like this evil brown powder. Faye's future was blighted, and there was no happy ending for her as she developed deep vein thrombosis by her early thirties due to her drug addiction. Her body is like a pin cushion from the needle marks, with her legs being the worst area visibly scarred. The trauma she suffered to her spine from the earlier car accident deteriorated over time and left her unable to walk. She ended up permanently in a wheelchair. Gina is now Faye's full-time carer, but despite her illness, Faye still needs to take metha-done. I sometimes see her pushing her around, which is not easy as Faye piled on so much weight from being immobile. Eventually Gina and Faye moved away down by the coast. I'm sure there is some hope for the both of them for coming to that decision.

Scott's world was getting darker, and to fund his habit, which was now getting heavy, he was riding around on a bike selling drugs for some dealer. I was awoken in the middle of the night by Scott, who was in an anxious state and saying the dealer was after him and was going to do him some real damage. My heart was racing as I knew this must have been serious for him to come to me, so I said: "Why? What have you done? What's going on?" He admitted he had double crossed the dealer. Scott had been ripping him off, along with selling the drugs he was using them himself, and he was now in deep trouble.

* * *

Right, that was it! I made an instant decision that we were getting out of here. Before booking any flights, I felt I needed to discuss my predicament with my friend Marilyn, as I needed a second opinion. I knew she had done a similar thing with her son, Stephen, in taking him to Benidorm in an attempt to thwart his addiction. She said to me: "Don't waste your money, Julie. It won't make a blind bit of difference, as all they will do as soon as they get back is be out looking for it again." It was, however, one of those things I had to find out for myself, and as Scott's safety was at risk, we were getting on that plane!

The only resort I could get at such short notice was Magaluf, in Majorca. So, in a midnight flit, Scott, Tilly and I went storming up the motorway to Gatwick Airport. What a relief to be finally getting out of the country, but in the back of my mind, the enormity of the problem remained. Upon arrival, we were transferred to a plush hotel for a two-week stay, and it was only then that I could feel safe and let my guard down to an extent. No one came forward to help; I don't mean for Scott, but for me. I was isolated and alone in fighting this monstrosity. In a situation like this, it's not always about the addict. The person helping them also needs support. Regrettably, it's that person who is usually forgotten and slips through the net, like myself, who was now drained.

While in Spain, we got Scott through, cold turkey, and after about five days he was clean from drugs but tired. He was eating like mad, which is the opposite of when they are on drugs, barely touching a bite. He was consuming three breakfasts, eating throughout the afternoon, then a further two dinners to top it off in the evening. He must have put on about a stone and a half to two stone in weight during the fortnight, which was great to see.

He still enjoyed a few pints each night, which was in moderation, and he didn't seem to be bothered about heroin, although I had a suspicion he had been offered cocaine, which he took.

Tilly was teasing him that he wouldn't be able to get drugs in this part of the world, but he piped up and said: "Not heroin, but I have had some Charlie." I wasn't as naive as I once was, and knew I couldn't put my complete trust in him like I had mistakenly done before.

When he did well, I praised him as encouragement to continue, but his denial was the biggest obstacle preventing him from permanent abstinence.

The sea and sunshine did wonders for him and Tilly, but as departure was looming, I became worried about returning to Swindon. Ideally, I should have stayed longer or permanently, but other responsibilities took over such as my job, and the bills that still needed to be paid. As we flew back, Scott seemed to be really happy to be going home. "I wonder why?" I asked myself. By the time we had landed, he was already making phone calls, and when questioned as to whom, he responded with: "Emily." He had just lied straight to my face as I knew that relationship had ended years before.

I had bought back some cartons of cigarettes from duty-free for friends and family, which I left in the boot of the car. No sooner had we got through the door than Scott disappeared, and I didn't see him for most of the night. I was frantic. The whereabouts of the cigarettes suddenly dawned on me, so I went to where I had left them, only to find he had swiped the lot. He must have pinched my keys when I went upstairs and put them back, so I was none the wiser. He had, therefore, chosen yet again to go back on drugs, and he needed to sell the fags for cash to buy heroin. I couldn't help but find his actions selfish, but he wasn't a selfish person. It's the addiction making him selfish, as all they focus on is what they need in that instant.

If only I'd listened to Marilyn I could have saved myself the best part of two and a half grand as he couldn't even stay clean for five minutes. I went looking for him all over the estate, knocking on doors and driving around in circles like a demented idiot. I waited up all night, but he never showed. So, I decided to go to bed, feeling exhausted.

A noise in the middle of the night disturbed me from my light sleep. I went down stairs and caught Scott just about to inject a fix. I hurtled over to him and demanded he hand over the needle, but he refused and said: "You don't understand. Leave me alone, mum." A struggle ensued, and I wrestled him to the ground, but he managed to escape and run off with the gear, not resurfacing again until the morning. I felt really let down and disappointed in him. My emotions were numb over what had happened, but he was my son, and he is an addict.

In my experience, all you can do is keep trying and trying in the hope they will 'get right' and be back out there building and fitting kitchens. I had this great weight on my shoulders, but I kept going with Scott as best I could, as I loved him and I wasn't going to give up. Maybe they just wake up one morning and decide they don't want this life anymore, which is what I was praying for every day.

A few years before, Scott had so much going for him. He was intelligent and interesting to talk to. He engrossed himself in books for hours, usually history or wartime literature. He loved drawing, and he never had a problem getting a girlfriend. But it was all fading away bit by bit. However, there were a few occasions when he would read, and through all the drugs madness, I got a glimpse of the real Scott. For that moment, he came back to me as the son I once knew.

Scott looking thin on drugs.

Scott and myself happy in Spain.

CHAPTER ELEVEN

Scott was complaining of feeling unwell, which wasn't that unusual for someone living his lifestyle, but this time it was different. He hadn't been long home when he went straight to bed, although he didn't appear to be under the influence of drugs. When he got up the next day, the flu-like symptoms persisted. So, he returned to bed. I had to go to work but drove back home in my lunch hour to check on him. Tilly, who had been in the house all day, said that he was still feeling rough. Tilly had advised him to call a doctor, but due to lack of strength and a headache, Scott was unable to make a phone call. She was getting impatient with babying him and told him to sort it out; she wasn't going to wait on him hand and foot.

I gave him a couple of paracetamols, thinking that would clear it, but I phoned the doctor regardless, and he turned up later that evening. By this time, it was apparent that there was something wrong with Scott's eye. It was watering and getting darker in colour. The doctor prescribed some antibiotics in the form of eye drops, believing it to be some kind of infection that would clear.

For the days that followed, I kept inserting the drops as instructed. But instead of getting better, Scott's eye just got worse. The same doctor who prescribed the medication turned up at the house the next morning to check on his progress, which surprised me. I explained my concerns that I was unhappy with the state of his eye and was on the verge of taking him to hospital. The doctor agreed with me and telephoned A&E to advise them to expect us, to avoid a lengthy wait. Staff examined his eye, and as the seriousness was evident, immediately referred him to an eye specialist.

The consultant took one look at the area and decided to inject a large dose of antibiotics straight into the eyeball as Scott's eyesight was fading fast. The amount of antibiotics was enough to sterilise a septic tank. Scott was then advised to stay in hospital, but he refused. It cumulated in a row with me, but he wouldn't have it and discharged himself.

Rebelling against clinical advice did him no favours as he was readmitted two days later with poison pouring out of his eye. Scott was attached to an antibiotic drip then transferred to a separate room on a ward, where he stayed for the next week. I would visit him in hospital every day. Only sometimes when I went into his room he wasn't there, and it would be a long time until he returned. I found this strange and was at a loss. Was he meeting someone bringing him the drugs, or was he out there getting them himself? The treatment hadn't worked as, after assessing the extent of his damaged eye, it was already too late. The specialist explained that due to his drug use over the years, Scott's immune system had weakened and was unable to fight off bad bacteria.

Your body holds an adequate amount of bad bacteria as it is needed, but when that bacteria travels through the bloodstream, it searches for a vital organ to invade, which in Scott's case was the eyeball. It could have attacked any of his other organs like the heart, kidney or lungs, which would have been life threatening. So, although we didn't feel it at the time, perhaps he was lucky. The specialist took the reluctant decision to remove the eye as he also explained that if he didn't take this step then the other eye could also be affected. If that happened, Scott could then be left with no sight or, god forbid, no eyes at all. The eyes are attached to the brain through the optical nerve, and had we not of stopped this in its tracks the bacterial infection could have spread to the brain, causing permanent brain damage.

All this was devastating and hit me like a thunderbolt. And as the operation was due to take place a couple of days later, I walked home, crying all the way. I felt this numbness like it wasn't really happening. Maybe it was my system putting up a defence mechanism in order to alleviate the situation. It never had entered my mind that this could happen because of using heroin. How naive. A song out at the time was Noel Barkley's "Crazy," which I kept hearing on the radio all the time. Whenever I now hear that song, it takes me back to what was happening, and I shudder.

I worried for Tilly as she was so frightened for Scott. It was not fair to her. She didn't ask to live with any of this. That night, we both walked around the house in silence then went to bed feeling nothing but upset. I woke up the next morning and for a few seconds I thought I had dreamt the whole thing, but reality kicked in: It was the day of the operation. I was at the hospital ward holding his hand. Scott didn't say much, just calmly walked down to the operating theatre when his time approached, and never looked back at me. That was it; his left eye would soon be gone forever.

For several weeks after, Scott had to wear a patch. A false eye couldn't be inserted as it was too early to put a foreign body inside the orbital space. I had to bathe and change the dressing on his eye every day, and after that was done, I would give him a big kiss. I can't tell you how painful it was to try and stay positive and reassure him that everything would be OK in the end. He would sit there in the living room most days, and as it was summer, I would be outside looking in through the patio doors at him. Again, it vaguely brought back memories of me looking at dad from the veranda window when he was recovering from his car accident in Australia, thirty plus years ago. Momentarily, I would glance in and feel scared, but not for me this time, for Scott.

I tried to keep him occupied until the false eye was ready from Oxford, and he did manage to clean himself up a bit until one night he slipped out of the house. Again, I drove around in my car searching, knowing full well he had gone out looking for heroin. He found it. Eyes or no eyes, it doesn't make an ounce of difference. I finally thought: "Enough is enough." I needed to get him into somewhere fast as I was dealing with an uncontrollable typhoon.

Looking back, maybe it was too little, too late. Addicts have to want to go to rehab. But when I mentioned it, Scott welcomed it with open arms. After endlessly searching on the Internet, I found a private rehab that seemed suitable for his needs and booked him in. It was a country manor house in Hastings called Narconon. It used some of the methods of Scientology to get people drug free, and as both Scott and I were desperate to try something different, it was instantly appealing.

He had followed conventional channels through Druglink in the past, and even though they tried their best, Scott never made much progress in terms of success. I was disappointed in their dealings as their knowledge was limited, and only after Scott lost his eye did a Drug Advisor suggest rehab, at £12,000 for six weeks. I knew six weeks wasn't going to be long enough for a cure, and at £12,000 a shot, I was in well over my head. I could probably raise the money for the initial term, but if he relapsed and had to repeat treatment I could never manage to afford that sort of amount on an ongoing level.

Narconon, however, charged £13,000 for unlimited care, meaning Scott was welcome to stay until he felt strong enough to leave, regardless of when that may be. Once you were a fully-fledged pupil—their name for a recovering addict—you could return as many times as needed if you relapsed, without any extra cost. I suppose I saw it as a safety net for him. If things deteriorated after leaving, he could just go back to rehab and begin healing again.

The day arrived for Scott to be admitted. The staff travelled down from Hastings to pick him up from the house. Off he went, aged 27, down the path with his bag and guitar. He suddenly stopped and turned to look back at me. I walked towards him and gave him the biggest hug ever, whilst thinking to myself: "He is so special, I absolutely adore that boy."

During his early days at Narconon, Scott became completely clean and was coming to terms with rehab life. It was six weeks until I was allowed to visit him, as prior to that he wasn't permitted to see family and friends, which is what I would have expected. I drove down on a Sunday. As I approached the vicinity, I found myself looking up at this very large, old, Tudor red-brick building. It had brown beams just underneath the exterior of the roof, and the sight was astounding.

I walked into the reception area with my handbag over my shoulder, but I wasn't questioned or searched, which surprised me. For all they knew, I could have been a dealer. I thought I would raise this with the manager of the centre once I was able to track him down. It was very large inside with long corridors and lots of rooms that imitated school class rooms; it also had a wide sweeping staircase.

I waited in an office downstairs to see Scott, and it wasn't long before he walked in and looked at me. Immediately, his weight gain jumped out at me. He was so much more pumped-up from all the regular meals and training he had been doing at the gym. He was also playing football in the large gardens outside and was proud to tell me that if any wood-work repairs needed doing around the place, they would ask him to fix it. He did admit that in these six weeks he had been struggling with homesickness and with being around 'strangers'. So, he was ecstatic to see me when the non-visitation period was lifted.

Narconon's methods are based on regular exercise and healthy eating and, in turn, developing a strong mind, which are all common sense things. After a couple of hours, I managed to speak to Eddie, the rehab manager, about Scott and how he was doing. He said Scott was coming along well and that all the staff were happy with his progress. The first few days were tough as he went through detox; his body had ached badly, and he felt low, but physically he got through it. I also mentioned to Eddie my observations about not being searched. I just believed this to be basic procedure so was a little uneasy about it, but it was soon cleared up. He was impressed with my suggestions and ideas and later offered me a job as one of the rehab managers, which was quite flattering to say the least.

Whilst at rehab, the area in Scott's eye socket had healed up. So, he was referred to Oxford specialist eye unit to have a prosthetic eye made to replace the temporary one he was wearing. Members of staff from Narconon accompanied Scott to the hospital to meet me and a lovely lady called Anita. She was an artist, a very rare profession, and responsible for matching his prosthetic eye with his remaining natural eye. However, the colour would never be a 100% match. She sat Scott down on a reclining chair and went to work on duplicating the colour of his eye, which was the most beautiful shade of blue. The actual pattern on the iris had to be captured as no two humans have the same. Everyone's is different. Anita went on to say she hadn't seen anything even similar.

At her work station, she carved out the shape of the eyeball from wax then manually painted the shape and colour of the eye, which was a blueprint of the real thing. The mould was then sent off to be made into a permanent ocular prosthetic, appearing to be made from porcelain but is actually a hard plastic that sits in the orbital space. Fortunately, not all was lost as Scott still had some muscle at the back of the orbital space, and he could benefit from some movement, though not as much as his real eye. It was the only differentiating factor between the two.

When an eye is extracted, you would think it would leave a dark gaping hole, but it doesn't. Remaining is flesh and muscle and nothing to look at that would cause you to be alarmed. It was devastating for me to watch my boy go through it, but he was still such a handsome young man. On the surface, he seemed to take it on the chin, but underneath I knew it bothered him as to whether he would still be found attractive to girls. Heroin was taking everything, and if he didn't change his lifestyle after rehab I wasn't sure how things would end up for him.

CHAPTER TWELVE

After several visits later to Narconon, I could see the rehab was doing some really good things for people with addiction. They held courses on "the way to happiness" and "controlling objects around you through strength of mind," which can be hard to grasp at first. I didn't fully understand the methods initially as they were totally opposite to the usual twelve-step recovery. Scott was doing really well and had made some good friends, people like him just wanting to get clean. But at times, these different methods were starting to frustrate him. There was no pussy-footing around. Narconon's ways are mind over matter. It was all about making the mind stronger and having the strength to say no so you can control a situation. You have to be focused, participate in exercise and take vitamins.

As Narconon was all about handling the physical aspect of addiction, they introduce the "student" to the *New Life Detoxification Programme* to cleanse the body. This is where they use the sauna for long periods whilst taking vitamins and Niacin, under the belief that when you take narcotics the residues are stored in fatty tissues within the body, which causes the cravings for drugs. The sauna and vitamins are an ideal way to draw the residues out of the body tissues; hence, no more cravings. However, it's compulsory that students undertake a full physical examination before they can be put through this treatment.

The outline of their regime for getting people substance free is accomplished through the following:

1. Exercise, preferably running to stimulate circulation
2. Prescribed periods in and out of a dry heat sauna to promote sweating
3. A specific regime of vitamin, mineral and oil intake
4. A sufficient amount of liquids to offset the loss of body fluids through sweating
5. A regular diet including plenty of fresh vegetables

Completing the detoxification programme can help the individual make significant improvements including:

1. An improvement in energy
2. Ability to think more clearly
3. Greater attention span and memory
4. An increase in feelings of general well-being
5. Greater awareness
6. Reduction of physical symptoms related to drug use including tiredness, depression, anxiety and irritability

The emotional aspects of addiction, once the physical symptoms are fully addressed, are assisted by the addict completing a series of life skills therapy courses. These are designed to help them confront the emotional effects of their problem and introduce the individual to a new sense of right and wrong. They help the addict to shift past the issues which caused them to start using drugs in the first place. The different courses in place which assist their treatment are as follows:

The Learning Improvement Course teaches the individual how to increase their reading and comprehension skills. It provides the student with tools to enhance their ability to gather and retain knowledge and overcome the barriers to study and learn, then apply that learning.

The Communication and Perception Course helps the individual to stop past impulsive behaviours and brings them in to 'present time' so they are not stuck in their previous drug-using patterns.

The Ups and Downs in Life Course is designed to help the individual to identify, handle or disconnect from relationships that may have negatively influenced them in the past.

Personal Values and Integrity Course is a course that introduces personal ethics to the student giving them the information that will allow them to improve choices they make in life with simple moral and ethical concepts.

The Changing Conditions in Life Course introduces the student to different areas of their own life and gives them a guideline on how to better their conditions.

With these practical formulas they can attempt to repair some of the damage they caused as a result of their drug abuse. Part of this course allows the student to examine and rehabilitate relationships with self, family, friends and society:

The Way to Happiness Course teaches the individual 21 principles that cover a moral and ethical code and way of living that results in a happier, more productive individual.

I got the impression they were not big on one-to-one therapy or using prescription drugs to overcome substance abuse, which is just as well as more people abuse prescription drugs than any other drug, especially where there is money to be made. Scott was looking really well, so what they were doing was beneficial and I couldn't complain. When it is someone you love, you are willing to try anything to get them right, no matter how many times they fail or how much money you spend. You can only do your best. Never knowing the outcome is the hardest part, but you have to keep going and rely on your tenacity. Anyone with a close family member suffering from addiction will go through hell and back again, so in the words of Sir Winston Churchill: "When you are going through hell ... keep going."

My life consisted of travelling down to Hastings on a regular basis, but this time it was with a feeling of sadness. That niggling feeling I had all those years ago about that little boy Simon had now become a bare-faced reality. News was circulating around the estate that Simon was last seen walking off with a bag on his shoulder several weeks ago. No one had seen him since, and the family were at their wits' end with worry. I felt very sad myself as I had known him since he was little and prayed he was OK.

Simon previously had been battling a heroin addiction and suffered some illness, but he had been clean for some time. He had done really well. The lack of work didn't help his confidence, and he had never really found his place in society. So, maybe he just wanted to go out there and find a new way of life, to reinvent himself completely. Scott thought the world of him, but I didn't tell Scott straight away in the fear it would concern him to the point of hindering his recovery. I just hope Simon is safe somewhere and finds what he is looking for.

One warm afternoon, Scott called and asked if I would drive down at short notice. Upon facing him, he seemed quite down and said he could no longer stay at the rehab and just wanted to come home. He also asked me for money for toiletries and tobacco, in the same sentence. Through my shock and bewilderment, I initially refused. But as I could see he was low, I stupidly gave him some money.

To lift his spirits, I told him that Zoe, an ex-girlfriend of his, was asking after him. Although she was a little troubled, she was not a drug user, so I tried to steer him in her direction. I was quite surprised when he said he didn't want to get involved with her again, and when I questioned him further, he divulged to me: "She's a bit strange because when we were in bed together she used to want me to strangle her." We looked at each other in quite a strange way and just started to laugh it off. Apart from the drugs, he had a healthy mind and wouldn't be interested in sadomasochism. I was also taken back as it's not something we would normally talk about.

* * *

My actions came back to haunt me as a few days later I received a call from the manager saying Scott had been found taking drugs. He was caught along with a member of staff, Spike being his nickname, who used to be a student and now was working at the rehab helping other addicts. I felt so guilty and quickly confessed I had given him money. But still a full enquiry was to be held, and in the meantime, Scott was suspended. Spike was dismissed on the spot after being interviewed. This meant Scott had to come home, which I dreaded as I didn't want him back in the old environment.

Scott had to write a statement explaining how the chain of events occurred, which is as follows (a true account in his own words):

My drug use started when I was in the sauna talking about it. I was in my friend Owen's bedroom discussing it when Spike came in and said he wanted to score but couldn't because he had trouble with the dealer in question. He said I could go out, and told me where to go, also supplying most of the money before saying 'as long as you score for me that was ok'. I went out and couldn't find the dealer so came back.

A few days later I decided to go out there myself without anyone else knowing as I still had the money. I managed to get what I wanted and went back to the rehab, giving Spike half of what I had. As I found out later some of the other students had used the drugs because they had put their money together and gave it to Spike, meaning there were more people involved from the start than I was aware of. The rehab found out through the testing programme, so a lot of the people got found out however, the centre gives you lots of chances as they understand very well how difficult it is to get clean.

Because Spike was a member of staff he was told not to return again. Even outside some rehabs, drug dealers are present but I know at the end of the day I have to take responsibility for my own actions.

CHAPTER THIRTEEN

Now back at home, I thought Scott could be vulnerable, and I felt anxious. Although I loved seeing him, I didn't want him back in the same area where it all began. In hindsight, I should have moved as soon as I found out about his habit nine years ago. But is anywhere really free from drugs? I ask myself. To my horror, and before I had chance to take a breath, Scott had gone out and scored. However, this time there was a sinister turn.

I was out shopping, but Dave's brother, Pete, was at my house along with Tilly. Pete was decorating the hallway, as he did jobs like that for me sometimes. Just as he was about to go home for the day, he stopped at the front door and shouted up to Scott: "Bye then. Bye Scott." An overwhelming, strange feeling came over him that something wasn't right, and he felt the need to go up to Scott's bedroom to check on him.

As Pete walked into the room, he saw Scott lying on his back looking stone-faced and turning blue, so Pete immediately called an ambulance. Tilly began giving Scott mouth-to-mouth whilst Pete was pumping his chest in the wait for the paramedics, who were quick to respond. The medics rushed in and took over, saving Scott barely in the nick of time. I arrived for the tail end, shaking with fear.

When Scott became conscious, he was most ashamed and embarrassed for the upset he caused everyone, especially Tilly as the effect the incident had on her was horrendous. I realised at this point I had put too much trust in him, but the reality was I couldn't.

After the traumatic event, Scott wrote in his journal about what had happened and how he felt:

My Diary

With all the experiences I have had in my life I have decided to write my day to day life.

Today was a lucky day, tomorrow I am due in court and the chances of me not going to jail are slim. I thought I should make it a day to remember, but unfortunately I would remember it for all the wrong reasons.

The day started with me making a cup of tea and trying to get my solicitor to call me back, which was not going well. I then decided to do some work on a plaque I was making for a friend's passing but the job didn't go so well so called it a day.

I made up my mind if I was going to jail I was going to use a bit first so managed to score after about an hour which was much longer than usual. When I left the dealer with the gear in my hand he said something about it was strong brown but I was already thinking about something else. When I got home I put away under half a bag on the spoon, but it felt like half a gram. I remember feeling the hit and then NOTHING just peace.

Then I came around or to put it correctly my uncle Pete pulled me back to life, I wasn't breathing they had to breathe for me. When I was resuscitated it felt like I was half dreaming and I could remember nothing of what I had done. My sister was there and my mum came back. Someone must have been looking down on me because normally no one comes in the room when I am in there on my own. But the thing that gets to me the most is the effect it must have had on my family, especially my uncle.

I can't thank him enough for saving my life and thank you mum and sister for being able to live and put up with me. And that was the 5th September 2006 another day in my life.

Signed S Rose

PS: I wonder what tomorrow brings …

* * *

Scott was worried about going to jail, as he was being prosecuted for attempting to steal a TV from a hotel. The downstairs window had been left open, and from the pavement the TV was visible. So, he thought it would be a quick in-and-out, something he could sell to get drugs. He got caught in the act and was nicked for trespassing and theft. And as he had entered commercial premises, the severity of the charge was higher than if he had stolen it from a shop. Things were notching up against him as he was also getting done for a home invasion. Again, the purpose was to steal, but he left empty handed, which occurred on the same day.

Scott had rarely been in trouble with the law as he wasn't an aggressive person and as he had his carpentry, it meant he could make his own money. This was probably a big part of the problem as it all came too easy for him, but on this particular occasion he got desperate for a fix and made a mistake.

Sitting in court, Scott was extremely anxious with thoughts of going to jail for the first time, but once the panel of judges heard that he was in the rehab system, although currently suspended, they were lenient. A female magistrate looked at me a couple of times and gave me a compassionate smile, as if to acknowledge my plight and my fight for change. The magistrates left the room together to confer about Scott's punishment and came back with a just decision. They saw it pointless imprisoning him and undoing the positive steps I had arranged, even re-mortgaging the house to raise the money, which his solicitor made known to them. Scott was sentenced to rehab, and we were both relieved.

The long-awaited call from the rehab came bearing good and bad news. Scott was not allowed to go back to Hastings, but they did offer him a place at their twin rehab in Holland. It seemed a bit extreme, but perhaps it was the new and refreshing outlook he needed to turn things around. It was ironic, as I wanted him in a different environment. I just never expected it to be over a thousand miles away.

We drove to Bournemouth Airport for his flight to Schiphol, Amsterdam, and even that was clouded with doubt as he disappeared for quite a while, returning with glazed eyes and overly happy without a care in the world. I knew he'd had a 'hit', which only reminded me I was doing the right thing in getting him out of the country. However, it was baffling as to where he got the drugs from as I had searched all his belongings before we left. This just confirmed how cunning addicts can be.

As he was about to go through the departure lounge, he stopped and turned round to look at me. Then he gave me the biggest hug ever. I threw my arms around him, kissed and cuddled him back before he went on his way to meet the staff, who were waiting for him at the other end. I walked back to the car slowly as my mind was in another place.

Scott arrived to a tall, yellow building that resembled a princess' tower with pointed steeples. It had iron railings around it, and stairs that led down to a cellar area.

On admission, he was taken to his digs, which were cramped to say the least as he was sharing with four other guys who were mainly being treated for cannabis addiction. Heroin and crack are not so big in The Netherlands; weed is their main problem, which is much stronger than the stuff you get in the UK, and the addicts are really messed up because of it. It's actually called 'skunk', and the legal highs are very dangerous to the body and mind, although you are not at liberty to overdose. Depending on the individual, it can cause psychosis, hallucinations and delusions after long-term use, and the Dutch rehabs are full of skunk users. When you see the repercussions from taking it you know that talk of legalisation is "no, not a good idea."

During his stay, Scott would go out for walks, go swimming at a pool located in another part of town, and, of course, use the sauna. The lady in charge at the rehab was called Joanna and was Swedish. She was a mature woman who would walk around the establishment wearing a black shawl.

Joanna was tall and she gave off an authoritative air whilst pacing the floors to ensure everything was in order and running like clockwork. All the students had the greatest of respect for her, and she had huge influence over them. Scott was very well looked after in her care. She even took him personally to the dentist when he complained of toothache. Treatment for extracting the tooth was free as all medical was covered by the rehab after I had made my initial payment to them.

With her staunch anti-drugs principles, including alcohol and even smoking, Joanna was currently responsible for leading the campaign in Amsterdam to have cannabis banned. Her stance echoed her intolerance of all mind-altering drugs, and she played a major part in fighting for complete abolishment. The availability of the stuff was so vast and was even mixed in with the ingredients of the cakes that are served in the cafes.

Joanna has suffered first-hand the horrors of drug abuse and what it can do to a family. She believes in tough love in a sense, but also that you should remain in contact with the person under strict conditions. When a person enters the rehab to do a programme, they have to stick to it. If he or she does use, then the centre should look at BOTH sides of the story. The person is of course wrong for reverting, but the centre may have made a mistake somewhere too.

* * *

(The following account is Joanna's beliefs in her own words):

Addiction is an ugly, ugly beast and it is very hard to deal with so I do tend to give people many chances. If a person wants to leave the rehab we do everything to stop them.

Prior to 2013 the rehab took about 20-25 people per year, they come from all over the world like Belgium, Morocco, Saudi Arabia, Oman, Canada but mostly Holland and the UK. In the argument of legalizing drugs—when alcohol was forbidden in the United States did that help at all? NO it led to big fights between various criminal groups. What needs to be done is more emphasis on drug education.

Children and teenagers should receive that more than once from people who know what they are talking about, for instance the people who have used drugs. Not the police, not some social worker, no the people who have done it and been there. My brother is a teacher and would always invite me to give drug education talks. After listening to lectures from Narconon staff the pupils would say 'no more lectures from the Police only you lot'. Another teacher said that quite a lot of kids would say after the session that they wouldn't turn to drugs.

Some worried parents would send the kids to Narconon for a drugs prevention week. This is proven to be very effective. One mother that sent her fourteen year old son to us told me what he had said to her 'I did not intend to use drugs but now I know FOR SURE I will never take drugs'. Another girl who started to experiment later became the leader of the anti-drug group at her school and is doing really well. So instead of wasting tax payers' time and money on stupid discussions on whether or not we should legalise drugs, that time and money should be spent on extensive drug education and given by ex addicts.

On the cannabis problem, things have gone way too far in Holland now. It was more or less legalized many years ago, with coffee shops selling it. Now it is being criminalized we are getting wild west scenarios in this country. Wherever there is a coffee shop at least you know where to look. There are some coffee shop owners who co-operate with us if we are suspicious of someone from the rehab who is using. They will tell us truthfully if they have relapsed and even phone us if that person shows up again.

This was the case in a certain drug area in Rotterdam near the station. If we were looking for someone who had run away for example, then we knew exactly where to look and the drug addicts and dealers would even help us find them.

Now, that everything has been "wiped clean" we have greater difficulty finding people, although on the other hand with the experience we have gained we have less runaways. So again, I am not focusing so much on fighting the coffee shops but doing all I can to make sure kids get lots of drug education so they never go down that road.

* * *

In Sweden, they have a great motto: "I say no drugs" instead of "Say no to drugs." They also organise all kinds of activities on markets, etc., to warn kids about drugs. If you say "I say no drugs," you are not judgmental and there is more room for a discussion. So, the emphasis should always be on lots of drug prevention. Instead of budget cuts in drug rehabilitation, look at the most effective drug rehabilitation centres and invest in those. That is my personal opinion.

Scott on the left during one of his sauna treatments in Holland

CHAPTER FOURTEEN

Six weeks later, I caught a flight to Amsterdam to visit Scott. I went alone as Dave said he couldn't make it due to his workload, although he did visit Hastings on occasions. He was just glad that Scott was in rehab, where he knew he would be safe and Dave wouldn't have to deal with the ups and downs of it all. He never coped very well with the situation.

When I landed there, Scott was with two staff members from the rehab waiting to greet me. Before we set off for the rehab, which was on the border of Holland and Germany in a place called Zutphen, an hour and a half's drive away, we thought it an ideal time to catch the delights of Amsterdam. We walked through the cobblestone streets, popping into the shops in the city to stop and buy Scott some clothes, then continued on to the Van Gogh museum and the Anne Frank house.

Antonio, one of the two staff members who had met me, wanted to visit his mother, Sophia, who lived in the town centre, so we made our way to her home. We arrived at a street which boasted big retailers with an international reputation like Cartier, along with rows of diamond houses, which were equivalent to jewellery shops in the UK but much grander and exquisite. Diamond tours are actually run so that you can learn how some of the country's best craftsmen polish and cut the diamonds.

The properties are situated near the old part of Amsterdam which are like something magical. However the frontage changed when reaching Antonio's mother's apartment. The front door was really shabby, and the age of the place made it creepy, especially when venturing up a very steep staircase. This was certainly a case of never judge a book by its cover, because when Antonio opened the adjoining door I was presented with this large, beautiful, flamboyant room.

There was a large marble dining table in the middle with the biggest candelabra in front of me, and as I looked up I saw the loveliest chandelier hanging from the ceiling all sparkling.

Expensive paintings hung on the walls, and the interior decor was period. The sight before me was like something I had never seen. We chatted with his mother and her Dutch boyfriend before Antonio sat at her grand piano and serenaded us with his playing. The way he played reminded me of Liberace's performance in his heyday, with both myself and Scott gladly embracing the experience.

Sophia made us tea in this large silver tea set, complementing the olives and fresh fish. She was a religious woman remaining faithful to her Italian heritage and was very concerned not only for her son but mine as well. A lovely and genuine lady who said she wished Scott well and would pray for him and all the young people at the rehab.

After the second time in rehab, Scott wanted to come home as he had now finished the course and was clean, although he could have stayed there for as long as he wanted. He had made some good friends, mainly guys who were from different parts of Europe. One guy he bonded with in particular was George from Bulgaria; he was there for marijuana addiction and developed a serious problem with it but was recovering. He invited Scott to go back to Bulgaria to meet his family after they got through the course. He was such a lovely person, and I encouraged Scott to go to broaden his horizons, but he didn't take him up on the offer. So, was his mind focused elsewhere?

The majority of the students had acquired part-time jobs in order to pay for their keep whilst at rehab, and I would have preferred Scott to stay and do the same. This was the case for Angus, a chap from Glasgow, who was the only other heroin addict at the rehab.

He was too frightened to return to his homeland as heroin was rife, with whole areas being completely drug-ravaged. He didn't trust himself to resist temptation and got a part-time job delivering milk in the morning and then on to a small cleaning job, handing the money over to pay for his keep. It was known Angus had no plans to ever leave, so management were happy to extend his lodging indefinitely, which is the same for others who permanently settle in Holland once they leave the establishment.

Scott was due home on 1st December 2006. When the day arrived, I drove down and picked him up from Bristol Airport. As we sat in the car, I turned to him and said: "Scott, I am really worried about you as I have had a premonition."

He turned and said: "What?"

"I woke up one night in a state of shock and pouring with sweat as I saw you lying dead in a coffin. I know it's a horrible thing to say, but if you don't try and find a way of changing your lifestyle, god knows how this will end."

I was trying to shock him, I suppose. He was taken aback with that and looked at me with surprise.

He said: "What? No Way!"

"Scott, please. I'm out of my mind with worry and, if anything happened to you, I don't think I could live without you."

He said: "Mum, I will be OK. I am 28 now. Stop worrying."

I took him home, and straight away he wanted to go out, which I was dreading. I said: "No you have to stay in with me for your recovery as remember what happened last time—you overdosed. As your body is clean now, taking a hit could kill you."

He went off regardless and never came home all night, so my concerns were justified as always. I kept calling and leaving messages as he wasn't answering, asking him to get in touch immediately. He did ring me back on the Saturday morning, saying he had met a girl, was spending some time with her, and was OK. He eventually turned up Saturday afternoon but didn't hang around long as he was going back out with this girl.

I wasn't really happy about it, fearing this could lead him to drugs as he was still weak, despite him saying he was strong. And did this girl even exist? His mood was happy and upbeat and his physical appearance looked healthy, but that could all change in an instant as he was vulnerable. By Saturday evening he confirmed he was still with this girl, whom he implied was local. So, if she was real, I wanted to meet her as I would be able to detect if she was a user.

I was due at work this day and didn't finish until Saturday evening. To get through the shift, I had to convince myself that he would be OK and that I should stop wrapping him up in cotton wool. Perhaps that was my problem. Scott did pop back later that night with this girl, so I felt slightly relieved that there was some truth in what he was telling me. She was thin, but other than that from first glance did not appear to be on drugs. Of course, I couldn't say for sure as he had met her at a friend's house, and most of his friends were now connected to drugs.

Alfie was one worthless creep who was like a magnet to Scott. He knew Alfie was a bad influence on him, so I don't know why he kept going back. I got the impression Alfie was the friend he was referring to, and as soon as I heard his name, my apprehension for Scott heightened.

Alfie came from a family of five children, three girls to begin with, followed by Alfie, then a younger brother, Jacob. They all grew up in a rundown council house on the main road which was clearly visible whether you were on foot or in a car, and the place was an eyesore. An old sofa was left on the overgrown grass in the front garden along with all the broken household appliances and overflowing rubbish. Alfie had been addicted to heroin for the same length of time as Scott, only he never had the opportunities Scott had, and the jealousy swirled around within him. He was a little sneak, like a rattlesnake that lurks behind corners waiting to mess someone's life up because his life was messed up. He was nice enough to your face but would stab you in the back once you turned around.

First thing Sunday, Scott went out again, but this time he said he needed some money as he was meeting his girlfriend. This pricked my suspicions as I knew something wasn't right, but I complied with his request as I didn't want him to feel doubted. When he returned in the evening, I had a long chat with him about his whereabouts and the company he was keeping, but my pleas were met with: "I'm fine. Just let me get on with it, mum." Tilly was also present but never really believed Scott, which is understandable as he had betrayed her trust once too often.

On Monday morning, he got up saying he had to sort some things out and was keen to get back to work. His attitude was promising, and in the evening he was watching a video. So, his mind was able to focus, and he was in good spirits. The following day, I dropped Scott in the town centre so he could search for work. I carried on into the office as I was doing a late-starting at 2 pm and finishing at 8 pm. It was not ideal, as I felt I needed to be around, but the bills had to be paid. All afternoon, Scott was on my mind, and I had this nagging sense of doom. At 4 o'clock, I called to check on his wellbeing. He reassured me he was fine and was eating pasta, but as the evening progressed, I couldn't settle and wanted to go home early but had to see it through.

When clocking off came around at 8 pm, I ran to my car with a pounding heart. As I raced up onto my driveway, the first thing I noticed was that the curtains were open. Not only could you see in, but the brightness around the room was enough to make your eyes squint. I opened the door and walked into the living room, sensing emptiness like there wasn't anyone else in the room. Until I looked down and saw Scott laying face first on the floor. I knew it was serious as I didn't get that feeling someone was present, the one you get when you can't see them but instinct kicks in telling you that someone is there.

I rolled him over in a state of panic and began shouting: "Scott! Scott! Wake up! Wake up!" His face looked swollen and a fraction blue, so I immediately gave him mouth-to-mouth, but as there was no response, I started doing CPR. I had completed a first-aid course, so my training automatically kicked in. I realised now why the room was so bright. When Scott collapsed, he dragged the curtain and the rail down along with him. He must have been holding on to steady himself.

My body went into overdrive, and the adrenaline was flowing through my veins at an alarming rate. Between my actions of pumping his chest and giving mouth to mouth, I called for an ambulance and then just kept going, trying to bring him round. When I got no life signs from him, I frantically ran out of the house into the street before making my way to the next door neighbours, Bob and Lynn. I wacked on their front door like a crazed animal. As Bob opened it, I burst past him going straight into the living room shouting: "Help Bob! Bob, it's Scott. I think he has taken an overdose as he won't wake up." Bob ran into my house and got straight to work on Scott's chest, but there was nothing.

The paramedics arrived and started attaching wires to his chest while also applying the paddles several times to shock his body. Still, no response. They also tried lifting him up into an upright position, but when they did so, I could hear the fluid building up in his chest. I knew that was not a good sign, and there maybe was no way back. I sat on the stairs in the hallway after a while, just listening to everyone saying "do this" and "do that." Then my brain went into a void like it wasn't real, and I was dreaming and not in my own body.

At this point, I froze as they prepared to take him to hospital in the ambulance and asked me to follow behind, which I managed god knows how. When I arrived, my friend Paul was already there waiting for me, and we were taken into a side room, which is when Paul made phone calls to inform the rest of my family. As they entered, they asked: "What's going on Julie?" But I couldn't hear what anyone was saying. The police were waiting outside the room to question me, but I wasn't ready to deal with that. I just sat in a daze of nothingness. The nurse walked in and just looked at me. I stared back at her and asked : 'Is … is he …?"

She said: "Yes, I'm sorry. Scott hasn't made it. We tried everything, but it was too late."

The shock I felt was overwhelming, and all I could do was sit and stare at the floor. That was it. It was all over. My only son dead due to drugs on 5th December 2006. My family didn't know how to react, and all I kept hearing in the background was: "I'm sorry, I'm sorry." But it wasn't sinking in.

Dave walked in with Tilly and said: "What is it, Julie? How is he? Is he dead?"

"Yes," I said in a quiet, shaking voice.

With that he just got up and stormed out with Tilly. His mind couldn't handle it. Tilly didn't say very much other than she hadn't seen much of Scott that day as she had been to the cinema with her boyfriend, Ben.

The sheer abnormality of what was happening was massive. The shock was surreal. As Tilly walked out of the hospital, I ran after her. She turned around and said: "You should have been watching him. He shouldn't have been left on his own."

Her words cut deep. I had tried everything in my power to help him, but at the end of the day it was out of my control.

We both felt guilt at not being there. It re-enforces the fact that you can't leave them for a moment when they are freshly out of rehab as it's when they are most susceptible to risk. Their bodies are not usually able to withstand the amount they were accustomed to in the past, which they don't realise. Hence, the reason they overdose. If only I had got back ten or fifteen minutes earlier, I might have been able to save him as he didn't look like he had been there long because his face and body weren't too discoloured.

Recalling the scene, there were some half-drunk cans of Stella on the dining table but no drug paraphernalia. Had someone been with him but legged it in panic, taking the gear, when they saw his intake had been too much? We don't think this was the case after all.

A police officer approached. He needed to investigate what had happened to Scott.

He said: "You must have been young when you had him. An addict, was he? I couldn't see any marks on him."

I almost found it condescending, as though he was implying Scott's death wasn't as important as it would have been if he were a grade-A student on the straight and narrow.

I replied: "Yes, he was an addict in recovery having just come out of rehab and was doing well." His tone really upset me, so I went on to tell him: "He wasn't just an addict. He was my son. Don't you under-stand? He's my boy, and a decent one at that, from a good family. He was well looked after but just got caught up with the wrong people and made a very bad choice which has now cost him his life. It's called HEROIN. You know, that horrible brown powder that destroys everything? He was also a hard worker, doing carpentry, and everyone admired him as he was a lovely person and good to his mum."

With that, the police officer was quite taken aback. He went on to say that his brother was an alcoholic, and it was destroying his mum and dad. I just sat there quietly for a moment and thought there are more people out there going through this than we could ever imagine. Scott hated that life and what it was doing to the family, but it's called 'ADDICTION'.

My dad, Stanley, wasn't at the hospital as he had gone out for the evening with his friends, but we didn't know which pub. I kept wishing he was there as he was the first person I thought of, although I knew really it should have been Tilly. I needed something to hold onto, and that was my childhood. I wanted to roll back to the beginning before being an adult, and dad was that part, the protector. He would never let anything happen to me, always wiping away my pain, but no one was in control of this, only Scott himself.

After I had finished speaking with the law, I asked everyone to leave. Paul offered to stay with me, but I refused, saying that I wanted to be with Scott. I sat with him for a while, just staring at him and wanting him to wake up. He just looked asleep. In my mind, I was talking to him, but no answers came back. I then decided I had to go home on my own. As I walked out of the building, I could hear this echo sound, then a suction, like the air was drawing me into something, but there was no wind. The sensation was like I was being pulled out of my world into another, along with a strong feeling that things would never be the same again. It was all over. Scott was nearly there, if only he could have put up more of a fight against this demon.

CHAPTER FIFTEEN

In the weeks and months that followed, I found it more and more difficult to get out of bed as the only escape I had from the pain was sleep. My sleep hadn't been too badly disturbed like it usually is when you experience turmoil as I was so exhausted mentally. However, when I woke up in the morning, reality hit me like a tornado, and I just wanted to go back to sleep as the pain was tearing through my body every waking minute. This routine went on intensely for six months, and all I was getting up for was to go to the toilet, wash and eat toast. I would then return to bed and try to fall asleep, hopefully into a dream world where I might just see Scott.

I became obsessed with watching life-after-death programmes on 'You Tube' as I was trying to find proof that there really was such a thing. I had always believed there was something more to this life, perhaps to comfort me that Scott's spirit was still alive. Why would a young human being go through life with all its trials and tribulations, and then nothing? What was it all for? I was trying to find some meaning to it because all I knew is that this person I loved so much had been ripped away from me.

I tried to hold onto what was around him shortly before he died, one thing being the last track he played on his CD. It was 'Iris' by the Goo Goo Dolls, which he loved, and after I listened to the words I realised how poignant they were in relation to how he felt. I sat in his bedroom with tears rolling down my cheeks as the song played out, as if it were his way of telling me how he was so misunderstood.

The lines were a reflection to the first hit he had taken when coming home from rehab. Maybe the impact after injecting was taking him near to heaven, and he wasn't ready to come back to the house.

The feeling wasn't long-lasting, but he didn't want to miss it this night. This is how I translated the verse into how he was feeling and the pleasure he got from the drugs.

The ending of the verse is how he was responding to taunts of being a 'druggie' as he was shouting out that he was more than that, and he "wants you to know who I am." I have had to come to my own conclusion because he is no longer here for me to ask. So, I have to try and get into his head and understand how he was feeling.

I didn't want to go out anywhere and face anyone as the thought of having to talk to people was something I really dreaded. When I did eventually venture out of the house, I was met with mixed reactions. Some would say nothing at all, and others would ask questions. I didn't have the energy to explain things, and it only added to my pain. So, I stuck to a closed-ended statement of: "Yes, I have lost my son, but I just don't want to talk about that right now."

The concern from certain people was real, whereas some were just being plain nosey. Tilly was going through something similar but expressed her grief in anger and lost her temper at the slightest thing.

"I am on my own now, an only child," she would say in a derogatory tone, hinting she blamed him for what he did and leaving us in this state. Again, I turned to sleep to block things out, always wishing I wouldn't wake up. Because I was burdened with hurt for Tilly and her suffering, it was a double blow.

When Druglink in Swindon heard that Scott had died, they contacted me and offered some free counselling. I would turn up every Tuesday for an hour-long session with a nice but inexperienced young lady, who didn't say a lot. She just sat and listened to me. The only input she would make was to say: "Why do you blame yourself? It wasn't your fault, so why do you feel so guilty?"

I am sure she meant well, but I just wasn't being heard, and I suppose I was looking for someone to analyse the situation and explore why it ended the way it did. Was it something Dave or I did that contributed to his downfall? Perhaps I wanted her to say it was, so I could be punished. I was the prime person supporting Scott, the one who suggested the idea of rehab, and through that was how he met his eventual demise.

This is how our sessions rolled around, and because they were not beneficial, I found it harder and harder to drag myself out of bed to attend. I think the centre lost patience with me after a few missed appointments and said they thought I needed more intense bereavement counselling, which they couldn't offer. My father was my rock. Apart from Tilly, he was the only one who listened and supported me through my dark days.

I was called in to have a talk with the local vicar about my loss, which was his way of giving me support. He sat me down and said: "What you have been through is something not all of us will experience, and I can't imagine what it must be like." It sounded like an old cliché at first as I heard that line so many times, albeit with good intentions. He then went on to mention the war days where mothers would wait anxiously for their sons to return home from battle, only to have some lose two or three from the same family.

This is tragic beyond belief, but it didn't register at the time, although it should have done. I had lost MY son, and that was all that mattered. However, as life went on, I could open my mind to other people's grief and identify with how they were feeling.

My employer for the last 24 years covered my long period off work. In these twelve months, aside from spending the majority of my time in bed, Tilly and I jetted out of the country on different holidays around the Mediterranean.

It was my outlet and a way of removing my mind and body from the pain I felt all around me. Being in different surroundings de-intensified my grief. I was unable to continue living in the house in which Scott died, due to the bad memories, so I sold up and moved to another part of Swindon. Looking back, I don't think it's a good idea to make snap decisions when something as devastating as that happens to you, because your mind is not clear. You need to give it time before deciding what to do long term.

One day in 2007, I was driving my car with the radio on, and to my astonishment this new release called "Rehab" began playing. I couldn't believe what I was hearing. Someone was singing about going to rehab, a thing so relevant to this period in my life. Straight away I thought of Hastings and Holland, and my thoughts took me right back to my experiences. So, I continued to listen intensely.

It was, of course, the most amazing voice of Amy Winehouse that belted out lyrics about addiction and her own personal struggles with both drugs and alcohol. At long last, the taboo of addiction was being voiced out, by a very brave young woman in the media for everyone to listen to. She commanded the stage all around the world with her trademark beehive, which brought her international fame. I was intrigued by her persona, and this fascination has stuck with me until this day.

CHAPTER SIXTEEN

A few years later, I was back into work full swing, and it appeared to be a normal day at the office until I noticed a missed call from my brother Mark. I thought this unusual, as he never calls me at work, and I had a sinking feeling that something had happened to my dad, who was now 80. After returning the call, I found out it wasn't dad at all. It was our Uncle Don (dad's older brother) and Aunty Dolly. Both had been found dead in their Spanish villa, and as dad was next of kin, it meant taking a trip to the Mediterranean to sort things out.

At first, I thought it could be too heavy for me, but surprisingly I bucked up. On arrival at Alicante, we were met by the local police and undertaker. We were told that Don and Dolly were found lying next to each other in the bedroom. She was bedridden but fell out when presumably suffering a heart attack. This may have caused him to overdose on his medication, which he used for dementia, and he subsequently collapsed beside her. They were 81 and 84 years old.

To add to this tragedy, their bodies lay undiscovered for two whole months, as they didn't mix with the local community. Dolly's brother first became concerned when he phoned the villa several times over Christmas. However, when there was no reply, which was abnormal as they were always home, he felt something wasn't right. He called the embassy in Spain, who sent the police around. As they approached the bedroom, the smell was vile, not to mention the millions of flies crawling up the windows and ceilings.

When the Police arrived, they had to break in as all the doors were locked. So, by the time we got there and entered the property, it was in a terrible state. Drawers were pulled out and left hanging.

The cooker was placed in the middle of the kitchen, and paperwork scattered everywhere. In a situation like this, the first thing the police look for is their passports, to identify them.

We couldn't find obvious personal items, such as Don's wristwatch and wallet and Dolly's handbag. All we were handed was his signet ring and her wedding ring. Other items of jewellery eventually materialised, but what happened to the rest we will never know. There were no obvious signs of a break-in, other than where the law enforcement entered, which had since been secured. So, one can only make their own assumptions.

We had to arrange fumigation of the villa, a funeral, and handle an estate worth an estimated one million Euros. In a funny sort of way, it was helping me with my own tragedy by keeping my mind occupied. It was no mean task. So, we had to appoint three solicitors in both Spain and England, taking several trips out there over a three-year period. Poor Don and Dolly, whom I had idolised. We were the poor side of the family compared to them, and we were shocked to see them end up like that. What happened? Why didn't they ask for help?

We held a simple service in the middle of a hot day, prior to them being cremated. We decided to bury their ashes in the garden of the villa. We felt it was what they would have wanted, as they loved the place. A few months later, Mark dug out a spot by the rose garden. Dolly's brother said prayers, and then we laid them to rest. It was a strange experience, almost like they were watching us, and even though I had never been there myself before, I could feel them.

One thing that was apparent was the presence of the villa itself. When walking up the long drive way towards the building, it was almost like it was looking back at you. In fact, Mark and his wife stayed one night whilst in Spain sorting out the legalities but decided to sleep downstairs. In the early hours, they heard footsteps upstairs followed by the noise of someone moving furniture. They just lay in bed and froze. My sister-in-law believed it was the spirits of Don and Dolly. So, there it was: always together in life and now in death forever. Very sad that the dream had come to an end one day in December 2009.

Going back to their early years, when they met, she was working in a local shop, and he began as an office clerk after coming out of the Royal Marines. Don first started courting Dolly's sister, but during this time, he and Dolly fell in love, and a relationship blossomed. They married soon after, he being 17 and she 20, and firstly residing with Don's mother and his siblings. Dolly wasn't from money but was a very classy lady, with an infectious laugh and style, always wearing pearl earrings. She wasn't conventionally beautiful but made the most of what god blessed her with, incorporating her curves and womanly buxom figure.

Her golden blonde hair was pinned all night, which would then produce soft curls that would be positioned under and rest just below her ears. She would spend hours every morning in the bathroom grooming herself to perfection, to the annoyance of the rest of the household as it prevented them from freshening up. Stanley would get quite frustrated and curse to himself as he needed to get ready for work. So, when she eventually emerged, he would say: "Good God woman, what have you been doing in there? I could throw you on that bed cos you need someone to ruffle that hair for ya."

The two brothers were like chalk and cheese, with Stanley being a bit of a ladies' man, but always a gentleman and a scholar who liked to get his hands dirty. Don, on the other hand, was more of a straight-laced kind of guy, a white-collar worker who kept himself pristine.

The married couple eventually purchased a nice suburban house in Maidenhead, as Don was making good money working for Wimpey Construction as an Estimator and was later promoted to Chief Executive. He was responsible for the materials that were sent abroad. He calculated how much was needed and then arranged the shipping, and he was making a lot of money.

Some of his work took him and Dolly to Nigeria, where she would help the children by teaching them English, to play croquet, and how to sew. She loved kids, so it was such a shame that she didn't have any of her own. She did once fall pregnant but miscarried at six months while living in Maidenhead, and never tried again. I don't know why as they would have made lovely parents.

After leaving Nigeria, they decided to settle in Spain, finding a plot of land in Moraira on which to build the villa they dreamed of. They did all the designing themselves, and from the kitchen window there was a breath-taking view overlooking the Mediterranean Sea. The building itself was white-washed, with huge rooms and an outdoor pool.

It was what they always wanted and what they had worked for, privacy being their preference. I got the impression Don wanted to escape life in the UK, but he never indicated why. There was no doubt in everyone's eyes they had the perfect life. But as time went on, and the older they became, cracks were starting to show, although we were not aware of any marital issues at the time.

Now they were retired, they spent a lot of time together, and as she had health problems, he spent his days looking after her. The marital trouble started when Don had an affair during his old Wimpey days. It was the usual story of the boss having it off with his secretary, which apparently went on for a long time before Dolly found out. She couldn't forgive him and threatened to leave but never did, instead continuing with the marriage feeling bitter and resentful. It got so bad that even a trip to the local shops would cause arguments and constant bickering due to her paranoia.

Dolly would check his receipts, and if the checkout girl's name was printed on the till roll, then in her mind she was the one he was cheating with, and it would lead to almighty rows. The whole situation had played with her head to such an extent that she had become eccentric and obsessed. All around the house, every bit of paper, including receipt books, and the backs of calendar note pads, had her writing on it. Some pages were as small as a postage stamp but had listed all Don's whereabouts with his comings and goings noted. The writing was minute but immaculately neat, and it was unbelievable how much text you could fit onto such a small writing area. It was all in chronological order, about what time he left the house and returned or whether he went off in a taxi somewhere. This is how she expressed herself, by writing everything down.

After investigating and searching relentlessly, no will was ever found. So, my dad, Stanley, requested me to act on his behalf, as he felt me being the best person for the job. The correspondence involved between the two countries was enough to drive anyone insane as you are dealing with death certificates, probate, powers of attorney and inheritance tax.

Our Spanish solicitor complied with completing the long-winded foreign tax forms. This wasn't just for Don and Dolly but their parents as well, in order to establish who their next of kin was, but obviously their parents were now deceased. My dad was his only surviving sibling, so he was next in line. The majority of the estate was swallowed up by legal fees and taxes, but what was remaining of both the villa and the money in their Spanish bank account was awarded to Stanley.

It was determined that Dolly died before Don as she had a blanket neatly placed over her up to her neck. They could not establish the timescale between the deaths, but as she died first, Don automatically inherited most of the wealth, meaning his family were sole beneficiaries, mainly Stan. The beautiful villa was eventually sold to the rich French guy who lived next door.

He bought it for his extended family for when they came to visit and completely refurbished it. Due to the Spanish economy being in dire straits and the ongoing recession, it would have been difficult to obtain a good price, but eventually it all worked out fine after a three-year legal battle. We would have loved to have kept it, but it just wasn't practical. So, there it was, all Don's hard work sold off in a flash.

Don and Dolly on their wedding day

Don and Dolly's beautiful Spanish villa in El Portet Moraira

CHAPTER SEVENTEEN

I had to carry on, which was very hard after Spain, and my thoughts were for my Scott. All I can remember is him always being there, which was nearly all of my life. Every now and then, a wave of thoughts about him enters my mind and I just buckle because of my loss. I get flashbacks of him as a little boy with his golden hair, blue eyes and cheeky smile. I have dreams of him that are so real and are such a treasure chest in my mind.

When I pass the housing estate, which Scott worked on, I gaze fondly at the white PVC cladding and soffits as I know it was all his handy work. I feel proud, but in the same breath it's upsetting seeing such wasted potential. Also, I have been deprived of seeing him get married and being a grandmother to his children.

How do you go on after losing a child? Well, I am still learning how to do that and probably always will be. When you lose someone, in time the pain fades and it gets easier, or "you learn to live with it." When it's your child, that pain never goes away, but you learn how to get on, or let's say you "have to" as it's make or break. The severity may lessen, but it never leaves you because they never leave you, not ever, which is something I hold on to.

I think of him all the time. He's just there in my mind permanently, and what happened, as devastating as it is, is part of me now. I have learnt that anything can happen to anyone at any time, so I never take anything for granted. I never thought I would cope again on a day-to-day basis, but as time went on, I got a bit stronger. One thing I will say is that the people I work with have been amazing and have definitely contributed to me being me again.

What has got me through are my two beautiful grandchildren, a blessing from Tilly. Sadly, they never met their uncle. And due to my love of music, I have reignited my passion for playing the violin and now am about to take another exam. As I have never been one for taking pills, I find relief in walking and swimming, although most types of exercise are de-stressing. The advice I offer to anyone that has experienced what I have is to find something that gives you an outlet. Something positive that gives you happiness. You will never feel normal again, but bear this in mind, it's a club no one wants to join.

Death affects people in different ways, and initially after it happened, Dave carried on with his life as normal. However, the underlying grief caught up with him a few years later, and he was unable to work because of depression. It is a far cry from what he once was, a wheeler-dealer always making money on the side as well as buying and refurbishing houses then selling them on for profit.

Dave did enter into another relationship, and the lady moved in with him for a year. In this period, however, she found him difficult to live with and couldn't put up with his ways any longer, so she called it a day. As he wasn't flush as he used to be, he needed to get a lodger in to help pay the household bills. This arrangement lasted even less time, as after just three months the lodger moved out due to Dave continuously flying off the handle. It was usually over petty things, such as food in the kitchen not always cleared away to perfection or something along those lines. Dave had lost control over the most precious thing in his life, his son. So, how do you get a grasp on things after that and carry on as normal? You just have to put one foot in front of the other and keep fighting.

After returning from work one evening, I was pleased to know that Rodney had got out of the spider web and was doing well after years of sobriety. He was running his own printing business and was the proud owner of two flats. He had a really nice girlfriend and a baby son. I was so glad for him but at the same time felt sad that Scott hadn't managed to overcome his demon. So, admittedly, I did feel bitter to a certain extent. All those lost opportunities which he could have had as he had the capabilities of making big bucks with his carpentry, and he didn't have a shortage of female admirers. I am not biased because he was my son, but I used to look at him and think: "You are a talented, lovely man."

The moment he started using heroin was the beginning of the end as that drug takes it all, and it keeps taking until there is nothing left of that person. Rodney appeared to be a success story, riding on a crest of a wave, as I had seen him on many occasions driving around looking healthy. However, things are not always what they seem. I bumped into his mother one day in the street, and she stopped to tell me that he had been badly beaten up in a nightclub in Birmingham.

He got tangled up in drug dealing, and immediately my inner voice was screaming out: "Please not drugs again. This can't be happening." It wasn't heroin this time but cocaine. He was either using the stuff himself or something went wrong with the deal, as the amount of coke he was handing over was less than it should have been. Once the drug dealer higher up the chain than Rodney cottoned on, he gave Rodney the beating of a lifetime and left him for dead. The guy that was with Rodney at the time, who was also another dealer, didn't give a damn how badly he was injured; he simply stuck his hand down his pockets to grab whatever cocaine Rodney had left.

He then did a runner without calling for an ambulance, as he was satisfied he had the drugs and that was all that mattered. When the emergency services eventually came, Rodney spent the best part of two months in intensive care, wired up to all sort of machines. He was literally at death's door. For the last few years, he had been giving off the impression that everything was rosy. However, behind the scenes, it couldn't have been further from the truth as he had got heavily re-involved in drugs.

He had actually lost his two flats, as instead of paying the mortgage with the rent he received from the tenants, he was spending it. All the money he made from selling his business, at a reduced price as it was close to on its knees, was gone. The girlfriend had left him, and he hardly sees his little boy. His whole world has disintegrated. There was no surprise that he had lost everything, and nearly his life, because that is what drugs do to you. I am not sure how he is doing now, but I sincerely hope he wins the battle with drugs. But do they ever cut free of that curse?

Alfie was another one from the past I had the displeasure to observe when walking under a subway recently. I barely recognised him, but when this fellow called out: "Hello Julie," I took a closer look and realised who it was. He was sat alone, and I can only describe his appearance as "near death." I would be very surprised if he lived for another year. It must be like fighting in a boxing match, and the same for alcoholics. You duck and dive, but if you keep repeating the same mistake it will eventually get you—"bang"—with a right hander.

I don't know how it will end, but I have written my story in the hope of being able to move forward and to help anyone battling an addiction, either their own or a loved one's. The world needs to know what drugs can do to a family, not just my family but all the other young guys' families mentioned in this story and beyond.

What drove Scott to take drugs? Maybe it was a combination of things. He was certainly loved enough. Did we all have a common denominator? Was it the neighbourhood we lived in, or were we in the wrong place at the wrong time? Or did it choose us? What is a model parent? All families have problems. If I really think about it, and based on what Scott first told me, is that: "The other guys tried it so I thought I would too—big mistake. I thought once I got tired of it, I could just walk away but it wasn't that simple."

As a parent, I will always feel guilty because that's what we do. Were we bad parents? In my heart I have to say no to that.

The day must come where we just can't sweep it under the carpet anymore. In my opinion, age thirteen is a good place to start educating the hard facts. We have all heard "say no to drugs." But the thing is, drugs make you feel good. So, as long as they make you feel good, there will always be someone around the corner to offer them to you. The only way to prevent it is education and knowledge. Prescription drugs and legal highs are becoming the big killers at this time. As a family, we never touched drugs or even had alcohol in the house, but I have the knowledge to know that one drug can lead to another.

Heroin will turn you into either a dog or a whore. Whichever way, it doesn't matter. The result is still the same. There is help out there, and lots of people make it through, but it has to come from you. Try and find some contentment. Draw on your family or support around you, and find something that brings you joy and happiness. There is a way through. Never give up.

"The drugs don't work."

This story is dedicated to my son, Scott David Rose.

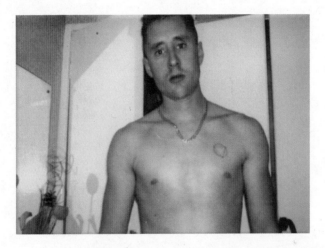

Scott aged 28, not long out of rehab,
who loved listening to "America" by Razorlight

"Don't hate the addict, hate the disease.
Don't hate the person, hate the behaviour.
If it is hard to watch it,
imagine how hard it is to live it."

MARILYN'S STORY

CHAPTER ONE

I have come to the conclusion that your life is mapped out, as I have done everything possible to be a good citizen, wife and mother to prevent the situation I find myself in today. HEROIN. Such a small word, just six letters long, yet causes such destruction. The year is 1998, and I am about to be swept along by an epidemic that was accelerating around Swindon, particularly Park North, a council estate in the east of the town. I have lived here since 1982, and the majority of those years, I would say, were happy. I class it as my home, and it is the place in which my children were raised. I still see many of the familiar faces around that have resided here the same length of time as myself, and their kids now are approximately the same ages as mine.

During the early 1980s when I first moved in, it wasn't an affluent place. People struggled to get by, but at the same time they took pride in what they owned and looked after their homes. Most families consisted of having three to five children, and back then it was very much hand-to-mouth as the welfare system was not so much available as it is today. As in most households, if in a two-parent home, only one would be working, and women tended to be "stay at home mums." I myself was a housewife and stay at home mum until my youngest daughter reached the age of three.

Single mothers certainly had it tough. Their income was very low, and one of the only few perks was that the kids qualified for free school meals. This is still in place today, which I fully support as healthy nutrition leads to a healthy body and in turn a healthy mind. A washing machine in the home was classed as a luxury and practically unheard of. You would often see mothers struggling with bag-loads of washing, draped over the pram or pushchair, taking it to the local launderette.

I guess you could say I was one of the lucky ones as I myself had a twin tub. One side would do the washing, and when the cycle finished you would transfer it to the opposite drum to spin the water out of the clothes. This is what my Saturday night consisted of in keeping up with the running of a relatively large family. I still had the daunting task of getting it dry, but we had three-month summers that were actually summers, not as bleak as the British weather is today.

Kids could be kids and would amuse themselves with things that didn't have to cost money. Marbles would be regularly played on the pavements outside the homes using the cracks in the concrete as the winning hole. They would get hours of enjoyment out of this simple pastime. Hide and seek was another favourite as they had the freedom to roam a long distance from the starting block. We didn't need to be so protective in those times as the thought of children being abducted was very far from our minds and not part of an everyday concern. Pre-adolescent girls would have no fear of doing hand-stands on the open green, allowing their dresses to fall around their ears, exposing their underwear. It was so innocent, and nobody batted an eyelid.

The park was a popular haunt with the slide being the main feature. It was at least 40 feet high, and you would have to climb about 100 steps before you got to the top. The graffitied roundabout was the second favourite piece of apparatus. The cheeky boys would entice each other to spin it with all their might whilst the girls sat on it unprepared. They would then be unable to get off so would have to endure it. Eventually, when stopped, they would stumble off dizzy and sick to their stomachs.

Today, this would be classed as a health and safety hazard as it was all unsupervised. But it was free, not like the enclosed adventure playgrounds nowadays. A real treat for kids was to be given 10 p to walk up to Spar, the only shop in the area, and choose a pic 'n' mix. You could get quite a lot in one of those white paper bags for that amount, such as jellies and white chocolate mice. The shop still remains, although it has been refurbished and changed hands many times over the years. It still does a roaring trade as it is used as a convenience store for when you have run out of that odd item. This was the simple era in which my kids grew up.

I'd just got home from working a 12-hour night shift at a warehouse distribution centre, packing and picking items for delivery to stores. The hours were long as you were continuously standing on your feet and walking up and down the long aisles. What made it worse was the constant pressure to fulfil unobtainable targets, and even then, if you reached them, it was never enough. My husband, Brian, and I were like passing ships in the night. As I was leaving in the morning, he was arriving for the day shift. We weren't academic people and always set our sights on manual roles, apart from the typing jobs I had done in my younger years. Professional success was not important to us; it was all about making a crust to support the family.

Maybe I was capable of more, but I didn't have the confidence to put myself out there. We always managed to get jobs at the same place, having worked at a door factory together before this company. It was heavy work, lifting and pinning fire door frames, and at only five feet tall, I was certainly made to earn my money.

* * *

They also made doors for council houses which were flimsy, being filled with egg boxes between the wood. Anyone in a temper could have put their fist straight through. Brian's role in his current job was being responsible for the salvage, which entailed collecting the redundant cardboard boxes from around the warehouse floor. They would then be gathered and recycled through a machine. The litter was also down to him to be cleared. He found this a nice little number as he was left to his own devices and not put under any obligation to meet goals.

There was a lot of back stabbing amongst the staff and management, which is typical in most workplaces. It was either down to boredom or jealousy if people were given more hours' overtime than others. I hated the place, really, but it was a means to an end, and I accepted it. Nothing was ever easy as it was a three-and-a-half-mile bike ride from our house to the factory. Our co-workers would often beep as they passed us in their cars. As we cycled in any weather—wind, rain or shine, through dark countryside, we would often get comments such as: "How the hell do you do it? You must be mad!" Unfortunately, a car was not an option for us due to the financial constraints of bringing up four children.

Brian could drive but hadn't sat behind a wheel of a car for over 30 years. So, he thought it was too late to start now. Everything I needed to do, like my grocery shopping, could be done using my bike, even if it meant multiple journeys. Quite often I would get carrier bags full of shopping whipped, and that would cost me dearly. I would have to leave them unattended in the front and back baskets and over the handle bars whilst I went from shop to shop. It was too much for me to carry them with me the whole time, so I had no choice. I was well known around Park North for being the woman on the bike.

After eating my breakfast, a healthy bowl of Shredded Wheat, I would go to bed, inserting my needed earplugs and putting on an eye mask to block out the daylight. I would then be brought back to semi-consciousness by my son, Stephen, shaking at my upper arm with persistence. "Mum, Mum, mum," he would say, peeling my eye mask up at the same time until I would eventually gather myself to a state of understanding. "Have you got a tenner you could lend me?"

This situation was becoming a daily occurrence. Why was he needing this £10 every morning and depriving me of sleep in the process? What was happening to my lovely 19-year-old son? This wasn't the same Stephen from just a few months ago. His appearance had become dishevelled. He didn't seem to be as hygienic as he used to be.

Smoking was also another bad habit he'd taken up, which was the strangest thing as he had always hated the smell. He'd always been quite vain, a very good-looking boy, who enjoyed giving and receiving attention from the girls.

Not only was it the way he looked, but his personality was changing. Instead of being mild mannered, he was agitated, even bordering on aggressive. This aggression escalated especially when asking for money and being challenged as to why he wanted it. Nothing could have prepared me for the next 12 years of hell I was about to go through trying to stop and cure his drug addiction. I look back and think about how my life began and how it had come to this. Is there anything I did wrong or could have done differently? I'm sure every mother of an addict asks herself the same questions.

Stephen, my handsome son

CHAPTER TWO

I was born Marilyn Ann, in Reading in 1945, to Gilbert and Eileen Ludlow. Bert worked on the railway as a district relief porter, progressing his way up to station master. His job involved working and travelling on the trains around the Southwest. He would also be the person to blow the whistle to indicate the train was departing from the platform. Accommodation, a station house, was provided for the family. Eileen left home at age 17 from the Forest of Dean, to find work in Reading, firstly landing herself a job as a waitress on the railway station. Later she was promoted to manageress on the side station where she met Bert. They knew each other for nine years before getting married in 1939. I came along six years later. I was an only child for many years, which I found a lonely existence, and as we always lived in rural areas, I didn't even have any play friends around me.

Myself as a baby with my father, Bert

Bert's motto was to get one on their feet before trying to cope with another offspring. My sister, Anna, did not arrive until eight years after me. Due to my childhood being like this, I always planned to have a big family consisting of at least six children. Bert took a real shine to Anna when she was born. She was favoured both emotionally and materially, even spoilt. I'm sure it wasn't his intention to treat us differently, but it did bother me.

At Christmas he used to dress up as Father Christmas, making me believe he really was him. He would bring a stocking with an orange in it, which was a real treat in those days as fruit was scarce.

My bath would be taken in one of those old-fashioned metal tubs, with water heated from the coal fire. We were middle-class, and although sheltered, I did have a happy childhood, attending Sunday school every week. I had to walk there and back on my own, which entailed a very dark pathway with overhead trees, but I was glad to mix. My mother was very loving and affectionate and had a real gift for baking. She would make the most mouth-watering blackberry pies with berries picked from the bushes in the fields. Cooking was her real passion, and she would busy herself with this as much as possible, as apart from myself she would not speak to a soul all day. She did, later in life, tell me how alone she felt.

All this food, usually made with real lard and butter, left her on the plump side, and being only 4ft 10 enhanced her overweight appearance. However, never once did her husband complain or make fun of her weight.

Her routine would begin by rising at 4 am to prepare a breakfast followed by toast and marmalade for Bert, seeing it as her duty. It was traditional for women to 'look after' their husbands. So, she would ensure he was amply stocked up ready for a hard day at work. The only gripe she would voice was the permanent fixture of bunions on the sides of her feet, which would stick out, making her need wider-fitted shoes. She would regularly visit the chiropodist to have them shaved off, only for them to return a few months later. A day of leisure consisted of cycling to Pangbourne for a picnic at the riverside. Bert would wear clips around his ankles to stop his trouser leg blowing into the chain.

When I was nine, we moved to a suburban area, paying 15 shillings a week rent. I would play with the doctor's daughter who lived next door in the corner cottage. I used to have a doll reaching two feet high, dressed in tailored clothing, and one of those shop tills with the manual keys. Finally, it was lovely to have someone of a similar age to share my toys with.

This little girl would later become Jacqueline Bisset, the Hollywood superstar, best known for her role in the film *The Deep*. I would often speak about her to my children, and thoughts of how different are lives were would come to mind. She was beautiful and wealthy with a successful career; I on the other hand was struggling to make ends meet, just a simple wife and mother, although the hardest job ever. We were worlds apart, but I wasn't unhappy.

I left home at the tender age of 16 to work in London as a copy typist for a year. It was scary as London was such a vast city, but I needed to spread my wings. Looking back, I realise this was quite brave of me, but I had an outgoing personality and believed in making the most out of life. I needed to move away from my childhood home as it was in the middle of nowhere, after we had relocated back to the countryside of Shrivenham from suburbia. It was so quiet, with nothing to do, a cottage-type property with nothing around but miles of railway track.

Anna and I had attended Bourton School, my mother transporting her on her bike, as it was a fair distance. The highlight of my adolescence would be to travel 20 miles to the nearest town for shopping and the cinema with my father. His brother, Len, retired from the army after serving in India, following in the footsteps of his eldest brother, who had been a high-ranking officer and had attended the Nuremberg Trials in 1945–49. Len married Ethel, and they had a child, Peter.

Memories of his childhood were etched in my mind as Ethel was a cold mother who believed children should be seen and not heard. The three of them stayed with us when Peter was around six. So, I witnessed his upbringing first hand. I was a teenager and can remember him being dragged out of bed in the middle of the night to be forced to urinate on the lavatory. He had a bedwetting problem, which Ethel hated and found disgusting so wanted to prevent it happening. He would cry out, saying: "I don't need to go. I don't need to go." But his pleas were ignored, and he would be made to sit there for hours, until he managed a wee. The whole time she would be scolding him, making him a nervous wreck so less able to go. Len stayed in the background saying nothing, which my mother could never understand as she thought Ethel's actions were cruel.

Len was a mild natured man with a flair for art, who painted a portrait of me when I was nine. It hangs in my living room. My features are clearly delineated, with big green eyes and neck-length hair. My ribbon is in contrast with the red diamonds knitted onto my green, Aran jumper.

Despite Peter's traumatic start he accomplished an Executive position at an IT Company and married Olive, whom he met through the church. After years of trying to conceive a baby, they underwent tests establishing they were both infertile, which doctors called a medical rarity.

From London, I came back to Reading after 12 months, lodging with a family known to my father in the city centre. I continued to work as a typist. In my spare time, I also tried my hand at a bit of clothes and swimwear modelling, as I had a slender figure. It wasn't serious. I just did it for a bit of fun as I always tried to keep in with the latest fashion.

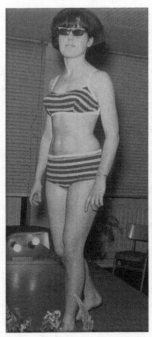

My modelling days

My hair was thick and black and usually long, but I did crop it on a couple of occasions when it was the trend. Age 19, I went out alone one night to the local dance at The Majestic Club and came into contact with Brian, who was a great mover due to him attending the Victor Sylvester Dance School in Liverpool. He was a dab hand at the waltz, quickstep and foxtrot. It was love at first sight for us both, despite us coming from two different backgrounds, but brought together as one. I found him to be very handsome with his stylish quiff, the fashionable hairstyle for men at the time, and he was dressed very smartly. He was a northerner but had come down south to look for work, managing to get a job as a furniture salesman whilst renting a bedsit with his brother. He had the personality to be able to sell ice to an Eskimo, which was in his favour as he worked on commission. He also served behind a bar a few evenings a week to keep his head above water.

We tied the knot two years later at English Martyrs Catholic Church, Reading, with Anna and my best friend, Margaret, at my side as bridesmaids. We then honeymooned in Yugoslavia (the part now known as Croatia).

My father became ill over a six-week period when he was aged 65, complaining of flu-like symptoms and a cough. By the time he was diagnosed with lung cancer, he was already dying. He had smoked a tobacco pipe throughout his adult life, and the fumes environment from the railway probably contributed to this. This was the first time I ever saw my mother shed a tear, as she did love him. He was a good husband, and provider, but wasn't always easy to live with as he could be cantankerous and liked everything just so. On one occasion during my teens, I can remember being woken up to the noise of him being on top of her with his hands around her throat. She had driven him mad with her constant snoring, and he snapped. I had to drag him off of her; otherwise I don't know where it would have led.

She outlived him by 26 years, missing him, but never moaned. Her outlet was to visit her sister Phyllis—an ex-school teacher who still lived in the Forest of Dean—for two weeks, twice a year. Both her sisters lived in bungalows next door to each other, which their father had built. It was a serene setting, as sheep would graze at the back garden-gate opposite to the entrance of the forest. She died at the grand old age of 91, her ashes resting in peace with her parents' at the local churchyard of her childhood home.

CHAPTER THREE

Joseph Brian was a war baby who grew up in the depths of poverty, one of eight children, including two sets of twins. His twin brother died at seven months from fumes after being left sleeping in a newly painted room. His immature lungs were just unable to cope with such a toxic substance. Just over a year later, one of the babies from the second set of twins also died. The reason for his death was unknown, so it was put down to cot death. Bizarrely, this was a boy also aged seven months. There were six children remaining: three boys and three girls that were orphaned by the time Brian had reached the age of five.

His father James (Jim) Cowell died age 41. He was remembered for his saying: "Oh sweet mystery of life I have before me" when getting up in the morning and stretching his arms above his head. He

Brian, on the left, and his siblings living in poverty

worked at the docks packing the fish as it came in off the boats. It was yellow fish called Finny Haddie, and he would take a few iced boxes of it to his family in Liverpool. He would travel by taxi at a cost of £1 each way, so not to allow time for it to defrost. His two brothers had been promoted to sea captains on the large ships and were pretty well off. Prior to this Jim was a clerk.

He was a hard worker and a hard drinker, although not an aggressive drunk. He was more happy-go-lucky. He would drink neat whiskey, which eventually caused him to develop stomach ulcers and lead to a painful death. Twenty months later, Brian's mother, Winifred, (Freda), died of pneumonia and a broken heart, also aged 41. She was of Irish origin of the name O'Connell and the daughter of a seaman, one of 13 children.

Jim and Freda were devoted to one another, and despite the poverty and bearing eight children, they had a passionate marriage and remained very much in love. Winifred, who used to work as a chambermaid at the Imperial Hotel in Blackpool in her younger days, struggled to cope with such a large family and made no secret of it. Although loving, keeping up with their everyday needs took its toll on her health. She would take the children, only half of them at a time, to visit her sister, Cissie, in Colwyn Bay during the school summer holidays.

They would play on the beach for hours, breathing in the sea air, taking advantage of their temporary surroundings. She found it difficult being away from Jim for even this short period and would write letters of affection to him regularly during her time away. When at home, the children were regularly fed bread and jam as that was all they could afford, and most food was rationed anyway because of the war, so there wasn't a lot else available.

Brian used to ask his father for a sandwich, made with margarine as they had no butter, just before he was leaving for the snooker hall. Jim would then shout up to his eldest daughter to make it for him as he was a kind man and wouldn't see anyone go without.

The siren would go off during the school day, instructing the staff and children to evacuate to the air raid shelter for safety. Gas masks were placed over their faces until they were under cover, and then all huddled together whilst listening to the commotion outside. One time when given the all clear, his aunt returned to her house only to find the bombs had blown the roof off and smashed all the windows.

The family all crammed into a rented three-bed terraced house in Heathfield Road, which was well maintained despite the lack of funds, as you don't have to be rich to be clean. Although as poor as door mice, his parents owned one best suit that would be worn on a Sunday with pride. Brian's paternal grandmother, who lived in a street nearby, kept her house spotless, even polishing the coal before placing in on the fire. Again, she and her husband had a loving marriage, both dying in their early 80s—he from a heart attack and she from arthritis.

After Jim's death Winifred deteriorated quite quickly and became very weak. She was bed-ridden with a constant fever and had to be cooled with a flannel throughout the day and night to keep her temperature down. Shortly before she died, a doctor was called to see if there was anything that could be done to prolong her life. Brian remembers him entering the house with his little doctor's case, but soon afterwards, she screamed out moments before she passed away. The scream was called 'The Rattle of Death' and could be heard down the street as the windows were all open.

That was Brian's last memory of his mother and has always stayed with him. Jim, Winifred and the two baby boys were all buried in a double grave at Fleetwood cemetery. Whilst the fate of the surviving children was being decided, they were taken in by a neighbour called Mrs. Bates for a few days. It was then arranged for the girls to be placed with Aunty Josephine, Winifred's sister, with whom she had been very close. Josephine never had any children and was a spinster. She made her living by working in the offices of a soap and farm food factory called J Bibbey & Son. The farm which was attached to the company was located some miles away, and with her being an employee, she was allowed to take the kids there for a day in the holidays.

Josephine and Winifred in 1913

Josephine's two brothers, who had immigrated to Seattle and had families of their own, sent her money at Christmas for the upkeep of the kids, as well as parcels which included clothes and chewing gum. Josephine wasn't an affectionate person, but she was fair, and underneath her cold exterior she did have a heart. By law she wasn't automatically given custody of the boys, so they were taken to an all-boys Convent Children's Home, which was run by nuns and was still in Fleetwood. When they were told that they were being placed in a home, Brian thought: "Home? This is my home," being so young he couldn't comprehend what was happening.

It was a strict regime, and if you dared misbehave, the slipper or the buckle of the belt was used as a form of punishment. The local tanner shop would make straps for the school which would then be applied by four whips on the palm of each hand. Another ritual would be to yank you up by the ear and walk around with you, making you taller. There was a child aged approximately nine called Dunstan who suffered a bed-wetting problem, obviously due to an underlying reason. He had no choice but to inform the nuns after it had happened, which was a nightly occurrence, and he was beaten on his bare buttocks. You could hear his yelps of pain echo down the corridors.

The diet consisted mainly of fish, which was caught from the sea opposite, accompanied by spuds, as well as the usual bread and jam. Johnny, the middle brother, once took a chance and asked for 'some more' after finishing his evening meal. His plea was met with a sharp slap across the back of the head, which was so intense it reduced him to tears, only being about eight years old at the time. I guess you could relate it to a scene from the world-famous *Oliver Twist* story. At Easter, each child was given an Easter egg which they were allowed to roll down the hill close to the Orphanage. This was one of the few happy events Brian recalled from his time there.

The schooling took place at the local Catholic Grammar, which was also Brian's religion before his parents died. The headmaster was named Francis, but you had to address him as 'brother'. Brian's sisters were schooled separately at Seaforth convent, with Josephine paying the private fees as she believed in good education.

Fleetwood is a small town and is well known for its trams that run to and from Blackpool. Brian remembers running alongside the track wearing hard, lace-up clogs, trying to jump on as it slowed down. He only ever had a ha'penny on him (worth about half a pence), which wasn't enough for the fare, and was ordered off by the ticket collector. He would be given pocket money for completing domestic chores within the home, handed to him by the matron. In a harsh tone he was told: "Do not spend it all at once."

After a two-year legal process, the boys were eventually reunited with their siblings, all residing together with Josephine at her large semi-detached house in Crosby, Liverpool. Her nephew, Seamus, was the illegitimate child of Cissie, which unfortunately warranted the term 'bastard' and was heavily frowned upon during these times. Seamus also moved in to help Josephine look after the brood. It would have been too big a task for just one person, especially someone who wasn't used to raising children. So, he became the dominant male in the house. Having contracted scarlet fever when he was 12, causing permanent damage to his heart, Seamus had avoided being sent off to fight in the war. He was classified disabled and given a medical discharge.

Josephine continued to work full-time, and her hobby would be to play the piano in the drawing room, where the family gathered to listen to stories of the "olden days." The kids were bought up with discipline, but not physical, as her voice and persona were enough to keep them in line. When Brian refused to eat all the dinner on his plate one time, she made him sit under the table all night. He was too scared to move and was found in the very same spot when the rest of the household arose in the morning. Needless to say, he always cleaned off his plate after that incident. As the O'Connells were strict Catholics and brought the children up under this religion, each of them were made to attend fort-nightly 'Confession' when reaching the age of 13. Josephine was also a very good seamstress. She would alter Seamus' suits, once he tired of them, to make short trousers for Brian's school uniform, which he teamed up with grey socks to the knee. She did it all by hand until she afforded a sewing machine once Brian reached 15.

I have vivid memories of Josephine whilst Brian and I were courting. She was a very stern woman who had nicknamed me "The Country Bumpkin." In fact, she had nicknames for all the partners as she seemed to resent them for taking "her" children away. Melville, Brian's eldest brother, who was the most intelligent of the bunch and achieved success as a headmaster later in life, had a gift for playing the violin. Once Josephine found out that he had become engaged to his girlfriend, Harriet, she threw the violin out of the bedroom window, smashing it to smithereens. As hostile as she was, all the children had the utmost respect for her as she had stepped into their mother's shoes.

Once the children reached their teenage years, Seamus began stepping out with a lady called Polly, who was 20 years his junior. Polly was very posh, her father being a banker, and Josephine would often mock her lifestyle. "We better brush the dog hairs off the sofa before she comes to visit" was her usual taunt. Polly was dressed in the finest fabric and was a different class to the family, but they married nevertheless, and it lasted for 30 years until his death, but never bore any children.

Brian and his siblings all eventually married and had children of their own, but the one consistency within each family was ALCOHOL. They each had a drink problem, and the ones who are now deceased died due to alcohol-related diseases. In my opinion, they used the alcohol to blot out the painful memories of losing their parents so young and the upheaval of being apart for a time.

My eldest two daughters and I did visit the "Home" when researching the family tree back in 2005. It was then a derelict building that was up for sale. It still had the stained-glass windows and the cross on the front door, with the words "+ Convent of the Sisters of the Cross and Passion +." The Catholic feel still remained, and it gave us an eerie chill.

James and Winifred   *Ellen, Brian and Janet walking to school*

CHAPTER FOUR

y dreams of having six children were not fulfilled, but I
was blessed with the birth of four healthy babies, three
girls and one boy. It took me two years to conceive my
first child, and I started thinking something was wrong. But then it
just happened. I had my first aged 26, a girl, Michelle, who was born
in Liverpool when we were living in a semi-detached house in the
Thornton area.

My first experience of childbirth, while excruciatingly painful for
most, was actually life-threatening. After having my legs forced open
and placed in stirrups by the Nuns at Fazakerly Hospital, forceps were
then used to pull her out. All dignity goes out the window when you
have a baby. I felt alone and afraid, as husbands were not allowed in
the delivery room during the 1970s, and the only pain relief was gas
and air. Ten days after the birth, when at home, I haemorrhaged all
over the bedspread and had to be rushed back into hospital. An emergency operation was performed to find that the afterbirth had been
left inside me. It was immediately removed, and my womb cleaned.

After recovering, nothing gave me greater pride than placing
Michelle in my silver cross pram with the huge wheels and pushing
her around. That pram served its purpose for all four children and
will always be a permanent fixture in my memories.

I was working in the Income Tax office, and Brian continued working as a furniture salesman, but we decided to sell up and purchase
a small newsagent in Anfield, a stone's throw away from Liverpool
Football Stadium. The Vendor, Mr. Moneypenny, said to us 'there are
wandering hands in here,' and would tap the would-be shoplifters with
a cane on the top of the hands and fingers. The living area was sec-
tioned off from the shop floor, but there was a hatch which Michelle

as a toddler could peer through whilst standing on a chair and watch us at work. On Saturdays, match days, we lost so much stock through theft. It made a real dent in our profits, so the business collapsed.

I almost felt I had two separate families, as my two daughters Michelle and Sarah came along in quick succession. There was then a four-year gap before Stephen and Rachel were born 21 months apart. Life was always a struggle, but I thoroughly enjoyed motherhood. We only had the first two girls when we decided to venture across the seas to South Africa on a one-year visa but hoping to gain permanent citizenship. Brian's brother, Johnny, and his sister, Janet, were already living there; so, we didn't feel completely alone. Johnny was a security guard for the world's leading diamond company, De Beers. He patrolled the merchant house in the heart of Johannesburg and the grounds where the diamonds were. Originally, at 16, he was training to be a priest, which I always found laughable. But when he came of age for national conscription, he was sent off to the army, bringing his church career to an end. He had the gift of the gab, and the women just seemed to fall for him.

He wasn't as handsome as Brian, but Johnny was tall and well-built. He was dating a local white South African girl called Dawn, who was madly in love with him. As he would not commit to her, she deliberately got pregnant, believing it would force him into marrying her. Instead, it pushed him the other way as he didn't take kindly to being dictated to. Not long after she gave birth to a baby boy, whom she named Johnny after his father, he left South Africa for the UK, seeing the baby only a handful of times before his departure.

He didn't hang around very long in his homeland as he got himself a ticket to Australia on the Ten Pound Pom scheme, getting stuck in with a job grape picking as soon as he arrived.

Shortly after his arrival, Johnny met Lizzie. She was plain, but he found her to be an easier going person, which he needed as he was high maintenance himself. He married her after a whirlwind romance, and they had four children. Johnny never returned to Britain, even for a visit, which he blamed on his hatred of the cold weather.

Dawn was heartbroken, and returned the matinee coat to me I sent her as a baby welcoming present. Johnny never laid eyes on his son again, and despite sending monthly maintenance payments until he was an adult, he managed to keep the child's existence a secret from his new family even to the present day. I never knew how he got away with it and had to make sure I never put my foot in it when Lizzie was around, which is not something I find easy as I have a habit of accidentally letting things slip.

Johnny was a bit of a cad. After our first introduction, he made no secret that he was in love with me. He propositioned me on more than one occasion to leave Brian and be with him. He did love Lizzie but said I was the one that got away—his one real true love—and I believed him. He was a confident, charismatic character, and I could see how he could sweep you off your feet, but he wasn't for me. I wouldn't have lasted five minutes with him as his drinking on a daily basis would have put us at loggerheads. However, even when highly intoxicated, he could still manage to present himself in a sober way and seemed aware of his actions, unlike Brian, who would be falling all over the place. The mere knowledge of knowing he was consuming this alcohol would have irritated me.

He was also very blunt in his manner, and at times I struggled to know in what context to take his comments, which again, would have put me on edge. I did tell Brian of Johnny's intentions towards me, but he dismissed it as a joke. So, I left it at that.

The journey to South Africa took three weeks by ship. We boarded at Southampton on the 'S A Oranje' destined for Durban, in 1974, at the cost of £800 all-inclusive for the four of us. The voyage felt like a lifetime, and all I can remember are the waves being very dark, deep and rough at times. I could not pacify Sarah, who was only three months old. She cried constantly, so much so that is was even bought to the attention of the captain. He actually paid us a personal visit to see what was wrong with the baby.

There was a swimming pool on the boat, and I would use it most days, weather permitting. Michelle used to amuse herself by running up and down the decks wearing her red strapped shoes. She used to like the echo they made against the wood.

I was very excited when the ship got close enough to see the outline of the country in the distance. It was during the time of apartheid in the 1970s. Everything was segregated between black and whites.

The beaches, park benches, toilets, even the pavements. There were visible signs displayed saying "Blankers Only" ("Whites Only"). There were consequences if you broke the rules, for both sides. This was a culture I was not familiar with. As soon as we docked, we were about to make our first mistake by venturing down the wrong path. We were quickly warned by a fellow countryman to stop in our tracks because it was a notorious area, and we would be either robbed or attacked. Suddenly the country's divide hit me, and I knew I always had to be aware of my surroundings as it wasn't a free land.

Brian, Michelle and myself arriving at Cape Town

At first, we stayed with Janet, but two families under one roof, for even a short period, resulted in problems. We got into an argument as I was accused of taking her tomatoes out of the fridge, but I fully intended to replace them. It was also a custom to have an African "house maid" who was employed to do the household chores and was very affordable, while Janet worked at the Airport preparing meals for the flights. I was also blamed for her leaving, due to me staring at her. I was told it made her feel uncomfortable. I thought it was more due to the amount of work that was put upon her and the way she was spoken to. Perhaps I did stare, but not intentionally, as it was all new to me. The atmosphere became so hostile that it was time to move on.

It was also quite an isolated place to live as it was in the middle of nowhere and surrounded by hills, making it very difficult to wheel up and down my silver cross pram. The nearest store was two miles away and was nothing more than a shed with shutters on the front. It was just a 'Tuck Shop' that didn't even sell the basics. The owner would park their car at the side. Janet's husband, Reg, also kept a gun for protection, and I didn't like the idea of staying in a place that was housing a dangerous weapon. After we left, he became further obsessed with safety and increased his artillery, even bordering on being gun crazy. Maybe he was just being over-vigilant, but he did live in a 'wild' area, not just for its notoriety of bandits but also for its animals. Reg even reported he had seen a lynx up one of the trees in his back garden. The lynx is the largest of South Africa's 'smallest' cats, which is fawn in colour, but still something to be wary of as it's likely to attack, although not as feared as a lion or tiger.

Michelle and Sarah as babies

We managed to find a small condominium with two bedrooms for rent, which suited us. I was enjoying the life, and we employed our own housemaid. He was an 18-year-old boy who took a shine to Michelle, who was aged three. He regularly reduced her to fits of laughter whilst taking the mickey and playing with her.

Sarah, on the other hand, was a whingey baby, waking me up every hour on the hour. I didn't realise at the time that she was dehydrated and needed water, but I kept feeding her milk. I often used to put her outside in her carrycot in the shade to absorb the tropical air. After glancing away for a short period, I would return to find monkeys hanging in the trees above. It was very daunting, and I'm ashamed to admit that I felt afraid to go and retrieve her for fear of being confronted. I always believed that this is where her love of bananas comes from because monkeys love bananas!

As our houseboy did the majority of the housework, which I was used to doing myself in England, I found I had a lot of extra time on my hands. I took advantage of the Durban beaches. The girls and I would sit for hours on the sand just watching the waves crash against the shore. I always tried to capture the moment by clicking the camera as I have a passion for taking photographs, doing so through every stage of my life. I never ventured into the water as it was shark infested because they managed to swim under the preventative nets and come close to the shore. It was normal to see people walking around with the loss of limbs, either arms or legs.

We did run into trouble on one occasion when Brian was the last customer drinking in a bar and was a bit tipsy. When he came back from the toilet and didn't seem to be in any rush to finish his beer, it aggravated the staff who were clearing glasses and tables. He felt the most almighty pain across his back, numerous times, as a guy began lashing him with a bamboo cane. Still a bit hazy, Brian chased the culprit down the street but failed to catch up with him. I don't really know what he intended to achieve, as he would have more than likely ran into further trouble, but I guess his natural reaction just kicked in. The next day he did go back to the bar to lay a complaint, but we never heard the outcome as to whether the person was sacked.

Johnny had befriended a black guy from Soweto, and Brian promised to let him have an old fire that he no longer wanted. Taking it to him was no easy task as whites were not officially allowed into the townships, and if caught you would either be arrested or beaten up by the locals. Johnny, who never did things by the book, drove there with Brian after dark, passing many shanty towns on the way. The fire was for winter, and as a favour Johnny fitted it on the wall for him under lantern-light. Brian said the whole adventure made him feel very uneasy, and he was glad to just get the hell out of there.

Our chance to begin a new life came to an end as Brian lost his job and was unable to find alternative employment. He had worked at a motor plant for four months on the computers, but not being a technical person, he didn't have a clue what he was doing. Management asked him to leave once the truth came out. We lived off our savings and decided to travel around the rest of the country by train.

We went to Cape Town, Amanzantoti, Johannesburg, and even to Rhodesia, now called Zimbabwe. We lived at each of these places for a period, renting cheap accommodation. Travelling with two small children and all our belongings was not ideal, especially when the journey could be up to 10 hours long. It was hot and stuffy, and the carriages were full. We used to place Sarah in the carrycot and then tie it to the overhead luggage rack, as room was limited. Talk about roughing it. But how could we not see what this beautiful country had to offer? Travelling is in my blood. By the time I reached my 60s, I earned the nickname "The Globe Trotter."

One of my dearest memories was when Sarah took her first steps on a picnic green on her first birthday, dressed in a white cotton frilly dress. One of my pleasures of having girls was that I could dress them pretty, and usually the same, just in their different sizes. I couldn't contain my excitement and let out a scream of joy, which didn't go unnoticed by passers-by.

It wasn't all sweetness and laughter. Shortly after Michelle turned four, she ventured into the deep end of a swimming pool unsupervised and without any band aids. I have to hold my hands up and say I did take my eyes off her for a short while, but it was long enough for her lungs to fill up with water. She was pulled out unconscious like a rag doll and had to have her chest pumped at the poolside in order to get the water expelled. I didn't realise what all the commotion was about until a teenage boy bought it to my attention. Luckily, she was revived, and I hate to think of the alternative outcome. I felt very guilty and it took a long time to work through my feelings of guilt.

At the same time our money ran dry, our visas were about to expire. We had no choice but to return to the UK. It did make me feel sad as I knew I could have built a good life in South Africa for the kids, what with the weather and the outdoor facilities. But it wasn't to be. You have to accept what you can't change.

As we were walking towards the dock to embark on the journey home, the year being 1975, a black man was following us, which I found a little unnerving. He finally approached and said: "Oi, mister, are you going back?" I replied: "Yes."

"Well," he said in a friendly yet concerned tone, "it's a good job because there is gonna be a blood bath over here soon."

His words rang true as just a year later there was a student uprising in Soweto with estimates of up to 700 people dying on the streets. This day, 16 June, is now marked as a public holiday, Youth Day, in the country in remembrance of the events.

Sarah and Michelle on the beach   *Sarah's first steps*

A day on Durban beach

CHAPTER FIVE

Penniless and jobless, we had to move in with my parents for a while. They had moved to a council house in Swindon. Anna, now 21 and single, still lived at home. So, it was going to be a full house. Not much had changed as she was still spoilt, being cooked a full fry up every morning which was delivered to her bedside on a tray. She was working as an insurance clerk, earning a relatively good wage, which she could keep all for herself. She would be inconsiderate in the mornings when getting ready for work, banging around, which would wake us up earlier than we needed to be.

A short period turned into a whole year before an opportunity arose for us to move up north, which was close to Brian's roots, and manage a second newsagent business. My dad lent us the money to take it over from the previous owner, Brian's sister, Ellen, and her husband. The business wasn't doing too well, and they wanted to get it off their hands. So, they sold it to us cheaper than the market rate. The flat above the shop was on a lease basis and we moved in. We took turns being on the shop floor as one of us had to look after the kids. It was situated on the main Wallasey Road, Merseyside, and a ferry ride across from Liverpool City Centre.

It was a seven-day-a-week job, with 5 am starts, as you had to be available for the daily newspaper deliveries. Our only respite during the two years we managed it was enjoying my parents and Anna visiting at Christmas times.

It was an old building with a cellar which held an infestation of rats. They couldn't expand from there into the main living area, but them just being there sent a shiver down my spine. We also had mice that were inside the property, and I was forever laying traps with cheese to stamp them out. I used to hear them scratching in the evening, and one time when I opened the airing cupboard, there was a horde of them in front of me.

Outside the shop was one of those old-fashioned machines, where you put your money in, turn the dial, and the sweets are available at the bottom opening once you lift the silver flap. Next door was a barber's, run by a man named Pooley, who was still cutting hair at 91.

The other side lay derelict, but prior to this it had been a chemist, managed by a gentleman in his thirties. One day, for reasons unknown, he travelled to North Wales with the intention of committing suicide. From that day, every evening between 8 and 9 pm, you could hear the same pattern of banging and see the lights go on then off, despite the building being empty. I felt the spirit was restless, and the property was haunted.

Sarah and Michelle with Eileen
outside our newsagent

Again, our efforts were dashed as business dried up. We weren't making enough profits to cover our overhead. Maybe the place was just doomed, as Ellen and her husband Phil continued to have a tough time even after leaving. Her third baby, a little boy, suffered a cot death at seven months, which was ironically the same age as her twin brother, whom I mentioned earlier. The tragedy was all too much too bear for her, and she hit the bottle big time. She neglected her other two children and her home as she just couldn't function properly. Phil, who now worked as a manager at the supermarket Quicksave, tried to keep everything ticking over, despite holding down a full-time job, but the situation took its toll.

He left her and took their two children with him back to the Isle of Man. His family lived there, and they were going to help him bring the children up. Ellen continued on a destructive path, seeking solace with other alcoholics at a local pub called The Boot. She lost the home and turned to prostitution to make her money. She was often spotted by members of her family sleeping on park benches, but you couldn't help her because she didn't want to be helped. Curiosity of their mother ate away at her children, and they asked to visit her one time during their estrangement. After witnessing her in a drunken stupor first hand, they decided not to see her again, but they did attend her funeral when she died aged 61 from an alcohol-related disease.

We had no choice but to return to my parents' house and quickly slipped back into our old routine. This wasn't how I envisaged my life, and we kept trying to change our circumstances. Brian was continually looking for work, but there wasn't much out there. Again, my father lent us £3,000 so we could purchase our own house and begin to move forward. We bought a property outright in the Rodbourne area of Swindon.

It was a mid-terrace, and we painted the window frames yellow to put our own stamp on it. Having some stability made us feel it was time to expand the family, and I fell pregnant quite quickly. Drew Street was the house that Stephen came home to after being born. I was conscious that the money was only ever a loan; so, we waited patiently on the list for council accommodation.

Persistence pays off, and things did go in the right direction as we were eventually accepted for our own council house by the time Stephen reached the age of one. I sold the house we were living in and paid back our debt, although it was a big mistake because that very house today would fetch a market price of £125,000. We were given a large three-bedroom semi ex-police house which sat opposite the Catholic school and church. It was surrounded by greenery and located on the outskirts of the estate, which made it more peaceful.

The birth of Rachel followed 21 months after Stephen's, and I felt that would be my last baby as the family was now complete.

Myself with Sarah and Stephen, with those gorgeous china-blue eyes

CHAPTER SIX

When doctors told me that I had given birth to a boy, Stephen Jason, I was shocked as I thought after having two girls we were prone to producing that sex. Now, at age 33, my only son, with white blonde hair and huge china-blue eyes, came into the world. He was the most handsome, angelic-looking child, enough to make anyone glance twice. I received comments a few times when at the local shops of how pretty he was, but it was said as if he was thought to be a girl. He was a joyous child, but he was lonely due to not having a brother, which he reiterated throughout his life. When he was three, he would ride around the house on this little yellow tricycle at speed, despite me telling him not to. He found this highly hilarious, and he would shriek with laughter whilst tossing back his tresses of hair. He would be wearing his 'Rupert the Bear' dungarees, which only enhanced his cheekiness.

Sarah, Michelle and Stephen

Stephen aged three

From the age of five, Stephen had to wear glasses. The only type you were prescribed back then was the old-fashioned looking ones with the thick brown frames; so, he was constantly called 'Joe 90'. He would find family holidays embarrassing as we had to use public transport, with a barrage of suitcases, kids and pushchairs. I never went out all year round, but I would indulge in a once-a-year break for a week at a caravan park. It was usually Weymouth or Devon, due to the calm, shallow water being safer for children.

The journey never went without a hitch, and quite often the train would take off with us on it, but the luggage still left on the platform, the battered brown leather suitcases and tartan plaid bags which Stephen felt ashamed to be associated with. We had to alert the guard, who then arranged for the luggage to be loaded on to the next train for us to collect at the other end. The sight reminded me of the suitcase in Paddington Bear, who I used to watch joyfully as a child on a black-and-white TV. He also accused me of talking in a loud voice for everyone to hear, but I think that I had become accustomed to speaking at that volume due to getting the attention of four children.

Sarah was always the lost child. More often than not, there would be a Tannoy announcement for me to collect her from the grandfather's clock on Weymouth promenade.

Stephen was the only one who had tantrums that could last for hours. Quite often he would walk off in the opposite direction out of sheer devilment or refuse to comply with a family outing. One day when at the beach, I bought him one of those whippy ice-creams with a flake lodged in it. Only moments after stepping away from the ice-cream van, he dropped it on the floor. Unfortunately, it landed in some little stones, making it inedible. He burst into tears as he was so looking forward to eating it, and demanded another one. I refused and started to walk away trying to defuse the situation. He then began screaming and shouting, drawing up an audience of spectators. Two elderly women who were within earshot looked at one another and said: "Oh, isn't that terrible." He got round me like he normally did, and I bought him another one.

I did make mistakes sometimes, as my mind was clouded due to the stresses of everyday life. Stephen was harder work than all the other three put together. Even buying him a pair of school shoes was a hassle. I always bought the brand Clarkes, which he hated as he deemed them old-fashioned. It was only lace-up or buckle style available, but he wanted a pair of slip-ons, the in-thing. However, I believed in comfort as they were made to measure. Every pair the young Saturday assistant would bring out, Stephen would refuse. He made such a fuss he reduced her to tears, as we could hear her crying out the back. She could not cope with him anymore!

He had a very sweet tooth, eating all the biscuits in the house before the three girls had the chance to have any. I didn't buy anything 'sweet' because I didn't believe in it, but my mum would bring around a packet of either Penguins or Kit Kats when she visited every Friday. That is why the girls were so annoyed, because it would have been a treat to have some chocolate. I guess he had always been quite selfish and I put this down to me spoiling him. Being the only boy, Stephen had everything new, but the others made do with hand-me-downs.

Witnessing Brian's behaviour when he was pissed always made Stephen feel uncomfortable, as Brian would babble a load of nonsense and become irate about world events. His hatred of Margaret Thatcher was what usually set him off. He was incensed by her treatment of the miners, as he remained patriotic to the North. He would wag his finger and say: "That's Thatcherism for ya. I want her out." However, like Julie, we did opt into her scheme and purchased our council house.

My old dad used to say when they would out for a beer together: "Brian you don't know when to stop." In today's terms, I guess you would describe him as a 'binge-drinker'. He wouldn't drink often, but when he did, it was always to a state of excess, which was the cause of most of our arguments. Whenever a special occasion would arise, such as Christmas, and I knew it involved alcohol, I would have to warn him for weeks before to stick to just two pints.

The first time we manage to afford to take the kids abroad, when our eldest was 16, Brian got so obliterated on Sangria that the kids had to carry him back to the coach. His position was the same as when you are about to give someone the bumps for their birthday. It was cringe-worthy.

This is the reason I never enjoyed our social functions as I was always on tenterhooks. I did, however, always allow him to go out on a Sunday afternoon for a couple as he worked hard and deserved some recreation. He would cycle to 'The Lady Margaret,' as he enjoyed chatting to the regular punters, and he would be home about two o'clock. One week, he failed to show up hours after the expected time of return. I began to worry after first being angry and saying to the kids: "Where the bloody hell is he?"

We never had a phone; so, I had to walk across to the red box on the corner to check with the hospital and see if he'd been admitted, but he hadn't. The police were my next call, and I was absolutely livid to be told he was currently sobering up in the cells after being picked up. He was found asleep on the curb with his bike lying to the side, bundled into the patrol vehicle, and carted back to the station. I marched home shouting again to the kids: "They've got him! They've got him! Well, he can damn well stew in it." When he began to stir, he didn't recognise his surroundings and thought he had woken up in Beirut!!

Stephen was nicknamed "bullet head" after being shot in the forehead with a rifle by an off-duty soldier, when he was playing at the lakes nearby at age 11. The squaddie was later dismissed for misconduct. The bullet was surgically removed, and he received stitches, but it did not leave a permanent scar. When the local newspaper got wind of it, they phoned me, and then sent a reporter around for an interview and photo. The incident was printed on the front page. When knocking at the door his friends now asked for "Bullet Head." The only other occasion he was hospitalised was for a hernia operation, during his playschool years. I told him it was caused by him shouting and bawling too much, bringing up all his energy from the gut.

Growing up, Stephen had a love of football; and like Julie's son, Scott, he was a ball boy for Swindon Town Football Club when he reached 12. The Manager of his team, Swindon Robbins, said he had a real talent, was a natural, and invited him to play on Saturdays, which he did for a year. By the time he reached the latter season, Stephen had scored 50 goals, most of them being outstanding, which got him promoted to captain and named 'Player of the Year'.

Stephen hung around with the same group of friends he had since infant school: Scott, Simon and Kevin. Kevin lived with just his mum, an older woman who doted on him and ran a good home. I felt she over-compensated with her protective behaviour due to her older two sons going off the rails, first with glue sniffing, and then both ending up in prison for burglary.

Scott was a well-turned-out boy, with both parents living at home who had good jobs. Like Stephen, he was small in size, and of similar appearance with his blonde hair and blue eyes. His curls were what always stood out to me. He only had one sister, Tilly; so, it was considered a small family compared to the others in the neighbouring homes. Simon was the 'thinker' who lived in the next street. Through their childhood all three boys had placid natures which I believe they inherited from their mothers, who were all gentle.

It was years later in his adulthood that I found out Stephen had endured a degree of bullying. I wish he'd told me because I would have done something about it. Maybe it was because I was working full-time and busy running the home that I never seemed to have time for a chat. As I'd had a sheltered upbringing, I never imagined things like this could happen, and I was oblivious.

Due to his quiet presence, Stephen was an easy target to mock, but it did also become physical. A group of boys grabbed him on the way home from school and tied him by his hands to a tree, using an old skipping rope. It was a planned mission from earlier in the day. After securing him they pulled down his trousers, leaving his underwear exposed. It happened in front of about 200 kids who were leaving the school gates, adding to his humiliation. The rope was so tight that he was not able to release himself. He was freed by a couple of girls passing by. He was a sensitive soul, and although he kept it hidden, this incident seriously affected him. He expressed that this had been the longest five minutes he had ever encountered.

Stephen had always been small for his age but had grown to six feet tall by his mid-teens. I don't know where he got his height from as Brian was no more than 5ft 6 in. At school, he was classified an average achiever, except for maths where he was top of the class. He had a good rapport with his teacher, Mr. Hopkins, but Stephen got caught mimicking him saying 'flee' instead of 'three' due to his Welsh accent when the teacher's back was turned. He did it just to fit in with the rest of the pupils, who branded him a swat. When Mr. Hopkins swivelled around unexpectedly, he ordered him out of the room. The teacher was a strict, intimidating figure who then pinned him against the wall. Stephen took the full force of his morning coffee breath, which absolutely stank, as Mr. Hopkins was shouting in his face.

Teachers were more heavy-handed then as rules against being physical where lax. Stephen's mischievous side really stunned me, especially when he fiddled the annual sponsored walk for charity. He completed two forms. One he handed in with the funds, and the other he collected for himself. As far as the school was concerned, they had their money and were none the wiser.

CHAPTER SEVEN

After leaving school, Stephen attended a carpentry course at college and showed true potential. I was very proud of him. My son was to become a carpenter and have the prospect of earning a good living. Regrettably, it all came to a sad end half-way through as he was bullied by the employees at D.W. Woodworking, a shop fitting company. It was a three-month placement that he had to attend during regular intervals over the two years.

On one occasion, he was thrown in a small cardboard box, and his legs were then forced in by tapering them together. They placed duct tape across his mouth as he was shouting for them to stop, then they closed the lid. He said it was like the effect of being alive trapped in a coffin. The four of them—Sid, Lev, Finn and Sankey—all began booting it with blows, mainly to his back.

They then proceeded to carry the box outside before throwing it at full speed onto the hard grass. Once sure they had gone, Stephen kicked himself out and returned to the workshop. As soon as he re-entered one of them said: "Make the tea Shirley," with no hint of remorse. This is the pet name they gave to him, which was a form of degradation. He was obliged to make the tea and got kicked up the arse when serving the tray of steaming hot drinks, causing them to spill.

The physical and verbal abuse was a daily routine. Another one of the rituals was to put Stephen in a headlock and run him up and down the length of the room whilst rubbing their knuckles on the top of his head. His hair caught alight when teasing him with a piece of burning wood as they waved it in his face. By accident, the fire did come into contact with him as he turned his head away, which they did put out in panic for themselves. The last straw came when hot tea was poured over his testicles, totally unprovoked and fully witnessed by the Boss. Their actions were simply overlooked. So, he walked out, vowing to himself never to return. I believe if these individuals had not behaved in this manner, he would have qualified, and his life taken a totally different journey.

I paid for driving lessons for Stephen's 17th birthday, but he wasn't being very sensible as he would drink four pints before getting behind the wheel. In fun, he would drive around the town centre at night teasing people as he passed. As they couldn't catch him, it was like playing a game of cat and mouse. He became a magnet for the police as they would spot the same vehicle going round repeatedly and would pull him over. He had been breathalysed five times, but on each occasion, luck was on his side as the alcohol had worn off by the time he was tested. One night, when the machine went straight to red, Stephen was arrested and taken to the cells. It was quite a while before they re-tested him, and by this stage he was now three points under the legal limit as the alcohol had left his body. Even the copper said he was lucky, then released him without charge.

Shortly after, Stephen was back in trouble for doing reverse hand-break turns in the road. He only did it to piss off the "boy-racers," as it blocked their access. The first time, the policeman let him off with a bollocking,. But when he caught Stephen red-handed the very next day, he wasn't so understanding. "Is your mate stupid or what?" he asked Stephen's friend. He then gave Stephen a producer and sent him on his way. To Stephen, it was worthwhile because he loved doing the reverse hand-break turns, and he pulled some wicked ones, nearly toppling the car over.

He was with a group of lads suspected of fighting after a night out, and although Stephen wasn't involved, it was a case of guilty by association. Arrested and taken to the station, they were then put into separate cells so they couldn't confer. Next door to him was an annoying guy complaining he was on fire, all night long. Stephen eventually told him to "shut the fuck up," as he grated on his nerves. Held for 19 hours, the lads took turns singing "please release me, let me go." They were released at different times to make their own way home, a five-mile walk. This is how Stephen spent his 18th birthday.

The year of 1998 was when my nightmare was about to begin. I was so unaware of the situation that was going to hit me. Having no knowledge or education on drugs, I went into it totally blind, and I was naive. The house now consisted of myself, Brian, Stephen and Rachel. Michelle and Sarah had since married and flown the nest. However, recently Michelle and her three young babies had moved back in for what was planned to be a short period. Her husband, an Army man, was sent for a six-month tour in Northern Ireland. So, Michelle handed back her house to the Forces, as he had signed off and was working his notice. It was going to be a real tight squeeze, meaning the babies would have to sleep in cots in the living room. It wasn't ideal, but families pull together to help each other through difficult times, and we just plod on.

As I worked nights and was not at home in the evening, I was told by Brian that Stephen, his friend Scott, and a few others had been coming into the kitchen and removing empty carrier bags. They all looked similarly unkempt in their appearance, but still the penny didn't drop. They would take three bags each and whisper amongst themselves as to what areas they were going to visit. We found this very strange and didn't know for what purpose these bags were going to be used. As I said previously, I was very naive and did not comprehend they were to accommodate stolen goods from convenience stores and garages.

Michelle, on the other hand, was suspicious of his behaviour and decided to mooch around his bedroom for any clues as to what was going on with him. Stephen's bedroom was relatively clean and tidy and not cluttered, which made it easier to snoop. She opened his bedside cabinet, which did not hold anything untoward. She then stood on a raised platform to view the overhead cupboards. SHOCK, HORROR, the evidence was there for the naked eye to see. Strips of tin foil stained brown, immediately raising alarm bells, although the full extent was not to be revealed until she opened the wardrobe. A clear plastic bag full of new unused syringes! I didn't know at the time, but this is what he called his "Party Pack."

There was no explanation other than heroin use. As the needles were not used, it looked as though the heroin was being smoked off the tin foil, which is called "Chasing the Dragon." This is the method most users use to introduce the drug into their bodies. Every parent, guardian or sibling finds out in a different way that their loved one is a user. For us, this is the way the truth was unearthed. Absolutely devastated was how Michelle felt. Her little brother was in a very dangerous and scary world. This was the worst drug ever and deemed as nothing but a killer. It rips apart your whole being and gets into every aspect of your life and that of your family. I can only describe it as like living in purgatory.

"No, no, no, I don't believe it. Heroin? There is no way Stephen is on heroin." That was my response when Michelle confronted me with what she had found. Even though the evidence was staring me in the face, I refused point blank to believe it. There must be another explanation, I thought, as I went into complete denial. I can imagine a lot of mothers reacting in the same way. The truth is too painful to bear. I waited for him to come home so he could tell me this was all a big misunderstanding. I did go in guns blazing as soon as he arrived but was quickly reassured that it was not his apparatus. He said he was simply holding it for someone. As unrealistic as it sounded, I believed him. I don't know if it was because that was what I wanted to believe or whether it was because I knew it simply could not be true. My son, so pure and precious; drugs would not touch our family.

Michelle was furious as I had bought his excuses so easily, dismissing his story as: "Oh, that's absolute rubbish!" All the signs mirrored a TV ad that she had seen. It was so harrowing that it had always stayed with her. In 1998, heroin use was not widely advertised and there was little drug education available; hence, the reason I did not know what I was dealing with. As the situation became very heated, I asked to see his arms, so we could lay it all to rest and prove Michelle wrong.

Stephen felt cornered. He showed his arms, and there they were: needle marks. You could not deny it. My son *was* using drugs. He had been smoking it for six months and then injecting it for the last three. How could he have been using for nine months under my nose, and I be unaware?

Smoking it only satisfies your cravings for a short period. As your addiction grows, you need the hit to get into your bloodstream instantly. Injecting is the only way to do this, but this is when you start on a path of being unable to come back. Stephen said the words my ears needed to hear: "I want to get clean, I want to get clean." Relief! Let's get this hiccup sorted and get back to normal life. I was under the belief that this was an easy, short-term problem to resolve. All he had to do was just stop taking it. How hard could that be? I now believed he was instantly cured.

It turned out he had experimented with street drugs at 16, starting with cannabis. A year later, he began dabbling in whizz (speed) and ecstasy at nightclubs and raves. They are stimulants which keep you awake, allowing him to party the night away. However, the hallucinations when coming down from the ecstasy made him feel very scared.

Stephen found an alternative passion to his carpentry after passing his PSV licence (Public Service Vehicle) the second time round. It was two weeks of intense training, leading to a job driving buses. To his relief, they didn't contact D.W. Woodworking for an employee reference, as he feared they would put a spoke in it. His learner vehicle was a "big old single decker" with a manual gear box. It was a nightmare due to it being so old and stiff, which gave him arm-ache for weeks. At first it was nerve-racking due to the size when manoeuvring it around, especially reversing. Initially he took pride in his role and told me he liked to give a good ride.

The passengers made comments such as: "You're a nice young lad, always polite. Not like these miserable old bastards today. They should get a few more like you." It touched him.

He was responsible for public safety and the handling of large amounts of money. Ironically, with his condition, it was totally the wrong place for him to be. He was getting paid a good wage, especially for someone living at home without any outgoings, but it wasn't lasting.

He kept coming to me for cash, and more disturbingly, he was spending the tender from the fares. This money had to be handed into the depot daily, but as it was short by £30-£60 a time, muggings here had to make up the shortfall. Firstly, he told me the money had been stolen from his station as it was left unattended, but soon he ran out of excuses for the missing cash. I had it out with him as to where this money was going. Drugs never entered my head as this problem was in the past.

"Gambling" is what he told me. Playing the fruit machines and losing. He had always been drawn to them when introduced during seaside family holidays. This stems back from the early age of five when going to the beachside arcade to play the "10p Silver City." You insert the coin and, if in the right spot, it would knock out a load of 10p's. Only Stephen being Stephen, he danced on the side of danger and cheated. Positioning himself at the side of the machine, he gave it a violent shake when the coast was clear. Handfuls of silver paid out, making an almighty noise and everyone in the vicinity aware. They all gathered over, and it became a grab for all. He told them to "sling their hook" as he was very protective about his money. Ever since that episode, he enjoyed the excitement and the thrill of winning, which spurred him to continue.

By thirteen, Stephen was sneaking into adult arcades around Swindon, but he was chased out when eyed by the cashier. He tried his luck at the next establishment, but again would be kicked out, begging to be let back in. But he was flatly refused as their licence was at risk. Sadly, this caused his potential football career to take a back seat. He even sold his season ticket at a cut price for use on the machines!

The catalyst of addiction was growing inside him, not just drugs but gambling as well. Professionals would describe him as having a "very addictive personality." It came to light he was also still using drugs. In fact, he had never stopped.

The money was now spiralling out of control, and my purse was continually open. I was handing out large amounts of money, quicker than I could earn it. Money dominated all of our conversations, but it was always given on the understanding he would pay me back. I was a fool. I believed that giving him money was the right thing, but all I was doing was enabling him to carry on.

As I funded his habit, he didn't need to take responsibility and face the way he was living. He was so desperate for money that the lies would become more and more radical. Lying was such a constant way of life that he even started to get confused by what the truth was and what wasn't. Addiction comes hand-in-hand with lying. Owing money to a drug dealer was the quickest way he could get a wad of notes out of me as I hated the thought of him being beaten up.

Stephen was falling deeper and deeper into drugs. He never bathed and had shaved his head at this point, which enhanced his 'pinned' eyes. This is one of the obvious physical signs of a drug user. He was also still driving buses, which frightened us to death. On the Sunday shift, he would go to his friend's house for a few tokes on his bong before driving off stoned. Was I to report him to save himself and others from an accident? Or did having a job give him an incentive to pull himself back? I feared that if he lost everything, he would go further down a bleak path. There was no instruction booklet. I didn't know what to do for the best.

The drugs were affecting his mind, and he was acting erratically. With a full passenger load, he would pull up outside the house, and the hazard lights would go on. Emerging from the driver's seat, Stephen would then say to everyone: "I won't be long." He locked them in, then proceeded into the house to eat his Weetabix. Michelle and I could not believe our eyes. After 15 minutes, he would return to the bus and speed off. He would also stop off for breakfast at places like Burger King, again keeping all the passengers waiting. Julie even said that one day she was so shocked to see this huge bus steaming down her small cul-de-sac as Stephen took it upon himself to go and see Scott at home. How the hell he managed to manoeuvre such a huge vehicle in this tiny space was beyond her.

CHAPTER EIGHT

(What follows is a true account extracted
from Stephen's personal journal, in his own words)

I was driving buses around bends and public roads at 40-50 miles an hour. The elderly people were holding on for dear life and were scared to death. I would let all the pretty girls on for free providing they gave their phone number when disembarking. This always made them pleased to see me as they got a free ride. My behaviour didn't go without reprisals and I was reported. Management pulled me in for an informal chat as they knew I wasn't acting normal. They suspected some kind of personality change for reasons bewildering to them.

Whilst breaking down I admitted to having a drug problem, regardless of what trouble it put me in. I was sat there "clucking" at that very moment as my body was in need of a fix, but managed to conceal it. To their credit the bus company gave me a month off to sort myself out, rather than sack me on the spot. They were clueless. "A month off" for heroin addiction was going to solve nothing. This is a demon and I wasn't ready. It was my crutch. I went back after this recuperation period, but nothing had changed. I was more berserk than ever, staying within no boundaries.

I hated the Wroughton route as you had to drive a metro van and being an old people's place, it was full of green plastic tokens. I despised tokens as they would go everywhere and had to be counted at the end of each day. It was a hassle that I couldn't be bothered with.

They could not be used before 9 o'clock in the morning, although some tried. I was having none of it and took great pleasure refusing them just to see the look on their faces. My mind had become damaged. Next came a catalogue of three crashes due to my head not being on the job. I went around the corner in a 43-foot-long Leyland going straight up the arse of the car that sat at a T-Junction, ripping the bumper clean off.

Secondly, I had loaded the fruit machine in the staff canteen during my lunch break with £50 and lost all track of time.

There was a tannoy announcement for me to get to my bus so in a rush I took off failing to follow safety procedures with the air pressure and buzzer. Due to my delay the bus that should have been behind me was now in front and was stationary at the flashing amber traffic lights. I put my foot down expecting him to move, but didn't, so went right up the back of him. Everyone on my bus incurred whiplash, which led to a suspension with pay as my excuse the brakes ceased was thrown out. Shortly after returning I hit the back end of a car as I wasn't looking when going over a roundabout, causing chaos.

The driver got out rubbing his head complaining he and his wife had whiplash. This also extended to their dulux dog which was sat on the back seat. Of all people he happened to be an off-duty policeman! The odds were stacked against me.

Management (Jock) had been patient with me, but my third crash resulted in a final written warning as this couldn't continue they had to take action.

Another near miss when pulling out in front of a speeding bus really shook me up. I left my seat and walked into the central reservation to gather myself. I put my arms over the railings. Then a female passenger approached me as a sympathetic gesture. I began waving my hands and swearing in frustration, but unfortunately she took it personally. She reported me so again I was suspended, which I saw as just another holiday, not a punishment. Her word held more clout than mine as she was actually an MP for Swindon. My misdemeanours always seemed to happen in front of influential people.

Totally high on drugs and completely off my face, I was driving an empty bus one morning in the pouring rain. I was very familiar with this route knowing of a puddle where the road dipped and collected water, measuring a foot deep. There was a suited man walking down the street with his umbrella and brief case and I had a sudden urge to drench him. I said to myself: "Right you are having it, you bastard!" Then I put my foot to the floor. I drove up at 30 miles per hour, knowing there was nowhere for him to run. I looked in the wing mirror as I passed, and observed a massive tidal wave go over him. I had the devil in me and enjoyed every minute of it.

A few yards up the road I stuck my head out of the window laughing and caught eye contact with him. I also made a hand movement whilst calling him a Wanker. The victim now knew it was a deliberate act. On the return journey, when approaching the same puddle, although this time on the opposite side of the road, I soaked two more unsuspecting members of the public. I deliberately drove diagonally across for a few moments to do the deed, before resuming to the correct side. I could have caused a head on collision and a lady passenger tutted and said: "That's awful what you have just done."

Back at the bus station the supervisor said: "Steve, you haven't just been on the number 8 have ya?" I denied it. He went on to say: "There is a bloke wet from head to toe, looking like a drowned rat. He is screaming and shouting, demanding money for the dry cleaning." A few other drivers witnessed the state of this bloke and were in stitches. After this I earned myself a reputation.

I continued working the same route, knowing full well the regulars didn't like me, so would taunt them. I deliberately went five minutes early on the rounds as I enjoyed seeing them run for the bus. If they hadn't quite reached the stop I would carry on driving whilst sticking my fingers up. I didn't give a toss. I thought it was funny. Another favourite was to pull up slightly past the stop so they would have to walk a few yards to embark—only to drive off before they got there.

Big time reports were printed in the local newspaper of drivers being rude and going before their time. The bus company then employed Inspectors to stamp it out. It wasn't just my driving that was dangerous. My conduct when stationary was also negligent. I was having sex on the bus with some girl whilst it was parked up at the depot for the night. I was interrupted by a supervisor, who started banging on the side window whilst I was doing the business. I felt really embarrassed to be caught with my pants down!

Rumours started to fly around the station and it gave the staff a real laugh to take the piss out of me. I had sex with a further two girls on board during my "career" which you could liken to the 70s comedy series *On The Buses*.

I was shocked when summoned to the office with the Union Rep to be told I was being taken out of town for a piss test. I knew I was doomed and my heart sank as I'd had some gear that very morning. Not surprisingly the results came back positive so was given the opportunity to resign, rather than be sacked. I did feel the company had been very supportive during my turmoil, and tried to help. Others would have kicked me out a long time ago. I was crying my eyes out when walking away very gutted and distraught. "No more Mr. Bus Driver."

* * *

*Myself and Stephen, who was
in the midst of battling his drug addiction*

With Stephen out of work and completely dependent on me financially, I thought a holiday would open his eyes to show him what else life has to offer. The four of us were off to Benidorm for a fortnight. Michelle and Sarah were annoyed as they felt he was being rewarded for bad behaviour.

They were law-abiding, and here he was being treated to a holiday. This is not what I was trying to do. To be honest, I didn't know what to do. It didn't get off to a flying start as we had to spend the night at the airport due to the flight being in the early hours. We had to travel up on the last coach, arriving around midnight. Trying to grab some shut-eye by sprawling out across the airport seats, whilst remaining in possession of our suitcases, wasn't ideal. Not to wake Stephen, Brian attempted to carefully retrieve something from Stephen's case, but Brian made himself look suspicious when gently opening the zip. A foot struck him in the stomach at full force, causing him to fall back and hit his spine on a hard surface. A fellow passenger thought he was stealing from a sleeping guy, until I screamed, 'That's his son'. The other passenger, realising he had been over-zealous, quickly apologised. It caused Brian back pain for the whole holiday, which was a shame as he needed this break away as much as anyone.

On arrival, Stephen had to go cold turkey, which took out the first few days. But once it subsided, he partied till the early hours, having nothing more than alcohol, and I could see the old 'him' once again.

The moment we got back to Swindon, he used.

The little black metro, with the central red trim, that I bought for Stephen to get him to and from work had become a drug run-around. You entered the car at your own risk. Even hardened dealers were scared when Stephen got behind the wheel. This is how he was funding part of his drug habit. The other part was funded by me.

Buying him this car was a mistake because he had no respect for anything. He was regularly fined and received penalties on his licence for speeding and parking it on zebra crossings. I had to pay to keep it taxed and insured, with high premiums due to the amount of points he had accrued. Stephen would carry drugs from A to B for dealers, and they would pay him with a bag of heroin. His habit at this point had increased to three bags a day, which was costing £30.

These ventures bought him back into contact with his childhood friend, Kevin, who had an addiction worse than Stephen's. Kevin was bad news, using both heroin and crack cocaine with his face showing all the tell-tale signs. He looked like death warmed up, with his naturally pale complexion and bulging green eyes from weight loss to his cheeks. Being around 5ft 10in, his slim build was made even slighter as he had swapped food for drugs. Kevin had mousy brown hair with a matching coloured goatee covering the end of his pointed face.

When taking Michelle's twin girls to the local shopping centre, Cavendish Square (Cavy for slang), in the double buggy, I bumped into them. They were demanding £20, and Stephen stated Kevin was prepared to drop the babies on their heads if I didn't comply. This is an insight as to how callous drug addicts can be, and a far cry from the ten-year-old boy that used to nurture his little Staffy dog. Kevin would knock on our door the moment he got home from school, with it standing beside him on a leash, which is how I can think of him in a softer memory.

Cavy was a run-down area and meeting place for the drunks and glue sniffers, who would congregate outside the off license. It was square in appearance—hence, the name—with the different premises forming this shape. In the middle were a few seats and an upward slope to gain access to the flats above. It must have been a noisy place to live as the pub below, The Cock Robin, was busy seven nights a week. I only used the place for my groceries as it was close to my home and I relied on my bike.

One afternoon, I came into contact with Julie, who also was dealing with a drug-addicted son. We both understood what the other was going through and how helpless we both felt. "Oh, isn't it a nightmare," were her first words to me. Maybe she could express to me what she couldn't to others, as she felt shame. Being Australian, she told me her perfect solution to the problem would be to dump her son, Scott, in the outback. It's desolate, thousands of miles of rugged terrain, so there would be nowhere for Scott to get into trouble. It also seemed appealing to me as we were both desperate.

The family was frantic. Stephen needed to be saved. Our relationships were fraught, and I was at constant loggerheads with Michelle and Sarah. They were unhappy with how I was handling the situation as no progress was being made. They felt I was too soft on him, that he needed tough love, but I couldn't do it. I knew my son and that he was not capable of being left to his own devices. They were sorry for me working all the hours only to hand over my wages.

There was also an element of favouritism as everything was going to him and nothing to my daughters. I didn't dare tell my husband about most of the money I was giving out, as he disagreed and it caused a row. He didn't understand why Stephen used heroin. Brian's exact words were: "Why is he injecting a drug which is used to kill pain, but he has no pain?"

It was agreed Stephen needed to be removed from the area and the familiar faces he was consorting with on a daily basis. We packed him off to Sarah's house as anything was worth a try. She and her husband were working during the day; so, Stephen had the run of the house to rest and recover. Sarah locked him in when she left, so he could not be tempted to return to the old haunts.

However, Stephen didn't cover his tracks and was caught leaving and re-entering through the downstairs window. He stayed two weeks, and in this time, Sarah found him to be hard work. He was demanding, and his dinners had to be cooked in a particular way, eating only certain foods. I guess I had pampered him.

The two oldest girls and I were off to the cinema to see *Titanic*, the must see film of the century. It was also nice to focus on something other than drugs constantly. I was so consumed by the stuff, it was as if I was using myself. In fact, as much as Stephen was addicted, I was just as addicted to curing his addiction. In professional language we would be classified as 'co-dependents'.

Just before we were about to leave the house to go to the cinema, a police car rolled up, and two officers knocked at the door. My chest tightened as I was told Stephen had been caught on camera stealing from a newsagent. Another murky world he was entering and earning himself a police record in the process. He was ruining his life and future. Why couldn't he see it? I felt like shaking him, but it wouldn't have done any good. As he wasn't home, they couldn't arrest him. We continued with our plans to watch the movie. We were not going to allow it to ruin another one of our days.

For just a few hours, I forgot my troubles and got captured into the story. I wished I was on the ship sailing away from the life I was living. The next day, Stephen was arrested and charged, finally ending up with a criminal record. This was the first of many convictions he accumulated throughout his habit. It was only ever petty crime, all relating to shoplifting. He narrowly escaped prison but was fined heavily on most occasions. Of course, I would foot the bill.

My bank card was missing. I was 99 percent sure who the culprit was, but there was an element of doubt, even hope, that I had lost it. At the bank, I was told transactions from my account totalling £200 had been made. My suspicions were confirmed, and I was now given the choice of prosecuting and being refunded or permitting him to

JULIE ROSE, M.L. & S.J. COWELL

get away with it. It was a hard decision to make, but for me there was no choice. I would never have shopped him as I didn't want him any further in trouble than he already was. I just had to be more careful with my bank card from now on. The thieving didn't just stop at me. Michelle had £10 stolen from her purse. She was saddened and disappointed as the amount taken was solely for a fix.

My elderly mother, Eileen, who was now widowed and frail, was living in sheltered accommodation. The grandchildren had always been a big part of her life. Stephen was the apple of her eye, perhaps due to being the only boy. He would often go and visit her and enjoy a cup of tea with handfuls of McVities chocolate biscuits. Her larder was always full of cakes, but now it was bought products, rather than home-made, due to her failing capabilities.

Whenever he asked her for money, she would hand it over without question or judgement. When I refused him, she would become his second source of funding. It wasn't big amounts, usually £10 each time. Over the course of his addiction, whilst she was alive, he'd received approximately £500. This is a substantial sum for a pensioner with little to spare each week. However, she ensured she had enough reserved to pay for her own funeral when her time came.

The heartbreaking part is that it wasn't only Stephen who would request money. After being introduced to her, a few of his friends would then visit her on their own and ask for the cost of a fix. They would sit with her long enough to have a cup of tea, which she served from a stainless-steel teapot into a matching china cup and saucer. It was quite a funny vision to see this elderly lady having a rendezvous with the local heroin addicts. I cannot deny they remained polite throughout. They pulled the wool over her eyes, disguising their true motive, and she found them to be pleasant young men.

Generosity was in her nature, always ensuring she gave a £5 tip every Christmas to the coal man, dustman, milkman, and even the hairdresser for her shampoo and set. There would be an envelope for each, neatly laid out on her embroidered table cloth, which she would gladly distribute. After her death, Stephen remarked that she was a proud woman, that's how he must have seen her.

Stephen and his metro became well known to the police as someone to be suspicious of for dealing. He had infamous status at the station, which left me sad as it was the opposite direction I had guided him as a child. I answered the door one evening to a handful of officers fanning a warrant in my face. They had permission to search the house, believing he was holding stolen goods. It was degrading to have to stand back and watch my home raided by the boys in blue. The embarrassment of seeing my personal possessions being handled made my toes curl.

They didn't find anything, and I breathed a sigh of relief, but I was also most surprised. Stephen was forever bringing back carrier bags of nicked brand-new stuff, which he would then sell on for less than half price. It was usually children's clothes from Woolworth or a fresh joint of beef, which could be bought cheap for a Sunday roast. Brian did have padlocks on all the bedroom doors to stop him hiding drugs as we were aware the house could be searched at anytime.

Stephen, distressed while on drugs.

CHAPTER NINE

It was time to get the professionals involved as I was getting nowhere. So, I booked Stephen an appointment at Druglink. After assessing him, they prescribed a course of methadone, and to give him every chance of succeeding, I decided to ship him off to Brian's sister, Marie, in Liverpool. I thought it best to get him away from everyday temptations and old friends. I had to get permission from the doctor to take a few weeks' worth of methadone with him.

I had kept in contact with Marie over the years by letter. She was the eldest of all the siblings and had run a pub for many years with her now ex-husband. My only critique is that she was two-faced. So, I was careful on what information I would divulge to her. She was different than her sister, Janet, who was up-front and told you straight to your face. Marie's trademark was the constant wheezing when she talked. There was always an odour of alcohol on her breath, and her cheeks were very flushed. To my belief, she was a secret alcoholic. On one occasion, curiosity got the better of me, and I hunted for her bottle. I never found it. Looking back, a drug addict staying with an alcoholic is not the best recipe for success, but I was desperate and needed a well-deserved break.

I travelled with Stephen by train and was met at Liverpool Lime Street station by Suzie, Marie's daughter, who had a gob like the Mersey tunnel. She was gunning for Stephen the moment he came into view, and her first words were: "Don't you dare mess my mam around. If you want 'smack', there's smack"—and she struck him across the face with the flat of her hand.

I felt sorry for Stephen, as she didn't even give him a chance. She just attacked him unprovoked.

I stayed for a few days before leaving Stephen in the 'safe' hands of Marie, who lived alone in her cosy terrace. I had molly-coddled him, and maybe that was the reason he couldn't stand on his own two feet. Marie took great pride in the food she served and was easily offended if you didn't eat it. I was, therefore, worried how he would cope with her meals, being so fussy. My break came to an abrupt end when, ten days later, I received a call from Suzie saying Stephen was no longer welcome. He only had to take his methadone and stay in the house. What could have gone so horribly wrong?

Marie, an attention seeker in my opinion, swigged down an ample amount of his methadone then went dancing in the street. She blurted out to the neighbours what she had done, so was in full comprehension of her actions. An ambulance was called, and the Paramedics checked her over whilst parked up at the pavement. She was given the all clear, but her children wanted her to have no more to do with Stephen. This was not his fault, but we were back to square one.

He was back in Swindon and using again as the methadone was not holding his craving. His addiction seemed to be worse than ever. He came home after just injecting a fix and sat at the kitchen table 'gouged' out, meaning he no longer even tried to hide it. Gouged is the term used to describe the effect once the heroin hits the blood stream. They go into a world of their own, drowsy and hardly able to keep their eyes open, as it's a depressant drug. Stephen said it was like being in a bubble, wrapped in cotton wool—warm, safe and protected. The true meaning of the word heroin comes from 'hero inside' because that is how it makes you feel.

Having a drug addict in the house creates a whole load of safety hazards. When looking in the airing cupboard for a towel, Michelle put her hand under an unused gap at the bottom. Something sharp pricked her finger, drawing blood. It was a used syringe. Panicked at the thought of contracting a deadly disease, we asked him if he was sharing needles. He said he had been with four other people.

Stephen had a fear of needles and had to rely on a co-user for injection. Michelle took a blood test for Hepatitis B and HIV, then waited six weeks for the results. They were negative, but the stress, worry and devastation caused was immense.

Not long after, Stephen came into the house with a friend, who was trying to persuade him to steal the microwave. His attempts to whisper failed as I could hear their conversation and automatically became guarded.

At the time, I was sorting through my white vanity case, which is where I kept my money in the house. In the case were numerous envelopes, one for each bill I had to pay, along with my correspondence. A drug addict seeing all that money on display must have been as tempted as a kid in a candy store. There was also a written list of everything Stephen owed me as I believed I was getting back every penny. This had now racked up to £20,000.

We were downstairs watching the evening entertainment on TV, thinking it strange Stephen wasn't sitting with us. He loved *The X Factor*, especially Simon Cowell, and would sit in awe of him. He felt a connection with him as they shared the same surname, but previously he used to hate the name. He felt embarrassed when revealing this information as kids would make mooing noises during childhood. However, when Simon came on the scene, he actually felt proud to own that name.

As we got engrossed in the programme, an almighty thud from upstairs made us jump out of our skins. Immediately, I knew it was bad news; call it a mother's intuition, but I just knew. Brian and I leapt out of our armchairs and hurried up the stairs to see what was going on, heading straight for his bedroom. We attempted to open the door, but only managed to do so a fraction as there was something blocking it. We kept pushing and calling out Stephen's name, but there was no response. His lifeless body, with his legs sprawled out, was stopping us from entering. We were able to manoeuvre his legs in the gap available and managed to clamber in, stepping over him.

It was evident to see that he had overdosed. He was unconscious with a syringe to the side of him. I was frantic, as I didn't have a clue about first aid, and I could only wait anxiously for the ambulance. On arrival, they put him in the recovery position and successfully bought him round. Thank god he was saved. He had been so close to death. The paramedics were under obligation to withdraw all his anti-depressant medication, as he was high risk of endangering himself. Stephen repeatedly overdosed throughout his habit, five times in total, and each time was a deliberate attempt to commit suicide.

I'd had enough! I was working my fingers to the bone for nothing. This curse was having a detrimental effect on Brian's health, and he'd been signed off work with stress. The company were not very compassionate, and the threat of dismissal was never far from our minds. It all got to Brian one evening and he verbally attacked Rodney, who was standing in our kitchen with attitude, talking a load of bullshit. Brian called him a "cocky little bugger while waving a finger in his face. The ginger Rodney ran off in tears as he didn't like hearing a few home truths.

I was depressed myself, and lost concentration, which caused mistakes. I rode my bike three miles into the town centre to do some shopping, locking it up on the racks. After returning with heavy bagsful of stuff, I realised I had left the padlock key at home. I sighed as it all felt too much, but I got the bus home and dumped the goods before bussing it back to unlock my bike. My relationship with my other children also was hanging by a thread. I had neglected them as all my time and energy was given to Stephen. It wasn't a case of favouritism. It's just the way it had to be to get him right. We had exhausted all avenues. The next step was rehab. I knew it was expensive and worried how we were going to afford it, but I was adamant he was going. I only hoped he would embrace the opportunity.

Luckily, we found a small facility in Weston Super Mare, a house converted into a rehab. I had to pay approximately £1500 up front, then they would accept his weekly housing benefit for the remainder of his stay. He had to be clean upon entry; so, he went cold turkey.

I never really understood this scenario because this requires specialised care, yet they are expected to accomplish this beforehand when being so messed up. There were strict rules. The consumption

of substances, including alcohol, and any form of intimate relationship are grounds for immediate expulsion.

Stephen's treatment was going well, and after several weeks he
earned the right to go into the town centre on day release. It was a
gradual process of obtaining independence and trust from the staff.
I spoke too soon, as he phoned to say: "Mum, I am waiting at the
station to come home, but there is a delay as someone has thrown
himself in front of a moving train." How sad that someone would take
such drastic action to end their life.

My thoughts then darted back to my own son, one step forward
and two steps back. What the hell was going on with his recovery? Apparently, a patient was caught with drugs, and although not
directly involved, Stephen failed to report it but was obligated to do
so. As harsh as it is, this is how committed you had to be. After a
three-month stint, he was back home and using drugs within days. It
was *Groundhog Day*, hanging around with the same crowd and doing
exactly the same things.

I wasn't giving up. We had to try something else. Michelle had
moved out as her husband had signed off from the Army, and they
settled into their own place. As it was now not so chaotic, I could be
more focused on the next phase. I enrolled Stephen in another rehab.
This time, it was a sought-after establishment, Broadway Lodge. It was
deemed one of the top three treatment centres in Europe. I was hopeful as this was the first time Stephen actually seemed like he wanted
help, rather than me wanting the help for him. As he had messed up
previously, he promised me to put in every effort. It was government-
funded, and we felt blessed as the cost privately was £26,000 for six
months. This scheme has since been abolished.

The treatment was five-star, ranging from the food served, which
was prepared by chefs and fit enough to be eaten by kings, to the
attentiveness of the staff and the different methods of therapy given.
A sponsor (an ex-addict) once said, which always tickled me: "I don't
know why they serve all this fancy food because when they get out
they would never cook it themselves as all they are going to do is open
a can of beans."

The ratio of patients to counsellors was one-to-one. The group counselling sessions were intense. They really had to look at themselves and delve deep into their background to get to the root of their problems and identify how they were heavily influenced by the past. They were allowed to be themselves, and if this entailed the regular use of foul language, it wasn't frowned upon, although it was under the supervision of a facilitator. It also consisted of reams of written work following the twelve step programme, which provided a supportive framework and coping skills to face up to fear and change. Each step is listed in layman's terms and has been in practice since 1939, when they were first published:

1. Admitting one is powerless over their addiction—that their life is unmanageable
2. Believe a greater power can restore sanity
3. Decide to turn one's will and life over to God
4. Make a searching and fearless moral inventory on one's self
5. Admitting to God, others, and one's self the nature of one's wrongs
6. Ready for God to remove these defects of one's character
7. Ask God to remove our shortcomings
8. List all persons one has harmed and be willing to make amends
9. Make direct amends to such people
10. Continue to take personal inventory, and promptly admit wrong
11. Use prayer and meditation to improve conscious contact with God
12. Carry this message to other addicts

Meditation was also a regular part of the healing routine, used to shift negativity. Stephen was in shock as he thought he was in there for a rest, but it was the opposite. Also, the amount of hugging was new to him, as I never did enough of this, expressing my love in other ways. At this particular rehab, they work on the theory that addiction is a disease and can be hereditary. Stephen then always associated his addiction with Brian, who was a binge drinker, and all of Brian's siblings were alcoholics. I also attended the three-day residential family programme they offer, to obtain a wider understanding of his addiction.

Stephen completed his six-month course, and the results were phenomenal. He was clean, healthy, and the old Stephen.

In order to sustain success once re-introduced into society, it is imperative to attend regular N/A (Narcotics Anonymous) meetings and say morning prayers from the Bible. Otherwise you are likely to relapse. Following treatment, the user is then transferred to a "dry house," which is less regimented than rehab with more relaxed rules. It's designed to get the recovering addict slowly back into the community with support, rather than being thrown straight into the lion's den. When at the dry house, the N/A meetings still had to be attended, which were held in Bristol and free transport provided. Stephen also completed this stage, making me so proud. To reward his achievement, we took him to Spain to my small apartment. It was part purchased with a savings plan that had matured, and the other half was on a loan. It had always been Brian's dream to own a property abroad, especially in Spain, and eventually retire out there.

After good efforts initially, Stephen became complacent and relapsed, which is exactly what he had been warned of. He wanted to be normal but would always be a recovering addict. So, he had to put in the ongoing work required. He was giving his sponsor, Paddy, the run-around by lying that he had gone to meetings when he hadn't. Paddy was dropping him off at the door, but as soon as he drove off, Stephen would scarper in the opposite direction. He also struggled to drop his old set of friends, which was vital for his recovery as they are a trigger. A sponsor is an ex-addict who acts as a mentor and gives support until the twelve-step programme is complete. I lived for the day Stephen completed all the steps, so he could then be a mentor to someone else.

Paddy stated that Stephen, who'd reached step nine, was the most difficult person he'd ever dealt with. He failed to comply, so Paddy ceased working with him, which elaborated what a horrendous job I had on my hands, and he felt pity. In his eyes, there were no excuses. Any addiction could be beaten through sheer determination.

Step nine meant that Stephen had got to the level of making amendments to the people he had harmed. He apologised to each immediate family member, including his Gran, for the abuse of trust and theft we individually endured. Trying to ease his conscience, we accepted his remorse, knowing it was a disease, and gently saying: "That's OK. We just want to see you get right." As he never had much dealing with his nieces and nephews, I was surprised to learn he felt guilt at not being an uncle to them.

In black and white, he freely admitted the theft he committed at popular high street retailers as well as companies he had worked for. Whilst on the buses, he stole £100 from the takings as well as threatening passengers. Under a temporary contract at a delivery company, where he worked shortly after his dismissal from the buses, instead of dispensing the parcels, he was stealing them. He visited both firms and openly told them what he had done, also offering reimbursement.

I actually felt proud that he had the guts to face responsibility stone cold sober and take the rap if they decided to prosecute. Being rude to people was another one of his sins as the drugs made him snappy and agitated. He was disrespectful in his verbal communication towards women and even begun pissing around at the gym, which used to have his full focus.

Time is the most precious commodity someone can give, which is why Paddy felt really kicked in the teeth by Stephen's lack of commitment. There is a waiting list for a sponsor, and Paddy felt his services could have been more beneficial to a willing candidate. He himself didn't start using until he was 37 and married with four children, but pressure took its toll and he reached out. Using crack-cocaine and living in squalid drug dens is what his life transpired to, but by his late-40s, he had pulled it back.

Paddy's drug lifestyle was the opposite of Stephen's, who still had all his home comforts and constant support, so Paddy couldn't comprehend why. He remarked that my house was like a little palace, decorated and furnished in cream. It was no wonder why Stephen kept coming back. Regrettably, Paddy's own daughter of 19 had just become introduced to drugs and was getting in way over her head on crack-cocaine. He was using all his skills to steer her, but it wasn't having much effect, as her own mind-set wasn't ready to listen.

It could have been a case of genetic addiction. Or was it what she had learnt from her father when he was using, like a continuing cycle? Paddy re-married to a recovering addict as no one understands an addict like another addict. At their wedding they were both tempted to have a tipple to celebrate the occasion, but they resisted as it could have been disastrous. He had been abstinent for 10 years and felt shocked that the draw was still there, proving you are never free.

Paddy also implied it was common for recovering addicts to form relationships with "church" girls as they were considered pure. He mentioned one guy called Dean, who was in his mid-twenties and very good looking, a recovering heroin addict, who also had a brother hooked on the stuff. When in the depths of my despair, I thought about this lad and his poor mother, who not only had one son on it, but two. How did she ever cope?

Dean got engaged to a girl associated with the church, but the rules of no sex before marriage really tested him. He loved her, but being celibate drove him round the bend, so, he paid for prostitutes, racking up debts he could ill afford. When he finally married her, it stemmed the problem as he could relieve himself and be happy.

Going back to Dean's youth, he began stealing when he was 14 years old as his habit started very early. He was a sweet-natured guy, but by the time he had reached his twenties, his addiction had even caused him to swipe all the Christmas presents from under the tree to sell on. Some would deem this as low as it gets, but his mother understood and knew it was without malice; so, she didn't hold it against him. She still cried, as she worked hard for her money, and the majority of gifts were for her grandchildren. His father was so angry and put the fear of god up him, so when Dean collected his next benefit payment, he replaced them in full. One day he was so in need of a fix that he was curled up on the floor spasming and fitting, so his mother sent his brother out to get him a bag of heroin. Being a user himself, he knew exactly where to get it from. As soon as the substance went into Dean's arm he appeared 'normal' again.

CHAPTER TEN

Stephen managed to get himself on another methadone prescription but was using heroin as well. He had abused his veins so much that they had collapsed. This was no good. We were going around in circles, and I myself was exhausted from lack of sleep. I was only grabbing three hours a day, from the mental stress of it all. Exasperated but not wanting to let the grass grow under his feet, I was sending him back to rehab, else nothing was going to improve.

There is a place for everyone in the cycle of change before finding a permanent exit. After a lengthy hunt around Weston Super Mare (the rehab capital in the south of the UK) by foot, I found an ideal unit. I am not a technical person, so an internet search was not an option. It was a Victorian property and ironically called Hope House, which left me feeling optimistic. I booked him in, but again, it was on the understanding he was clean upon entry, a hurdle I would have to overcome.

Taking advantage of my dilemma, Stephen insisted we go to a hot country to ease his cold turkey symptoms, as the sea and sun would distract him. I guess I felt emotionally blackmailed, as I would have done anything for a cure. I took enough methadone to pacify the aches and pains, which would be out of his system by the time he was admitted. The only snag is that methadone is forbidden through customs at the airport, but he was adamant he couldn't cope without it.

I was willing to take the risk and smuggle it in my suitcase. Better me than him, as I didn't look like a "usual suspect." To disguise it, I poured it into an empty bottle of Night Nurse, the flu medication, because Night Nurse and methadone are both green in colour. When the girls heard what I intended they begged me not to. But I was desperate, and nothing was going to stop me. I had as much tenacity running through my blood as he had heroin through his.

Michelle, myself & Sarah enjoying an evening out

We boarded for Tenerife, but it wasn't quite the holiday Stephen had planned as he suffered with the detoxing. The shakes were particularly violent, so much so I had to sit on top of his legs. He also had a severe case of piles, which is one of the main side effects from heroin as it causes constipation. Once it had all died down, we lazed around the pool together as we had a good relationship and were close. We returned to the UK on Saturday because he was due to go to rehab the next day. I wanted the smallest gap possible between this transition period to avoid the opportunity to score.

An excuse to pop out didn't cause me concern, but lo and behold, he abused my trust and headed straight for the dealer. I was at my wits' end. All my efforts had been fruitless, and I'd wasted even more money. It was all just a ploy to get a free holiday out of me. I went to the rehab anyway explaining my predicament to the manager whilst standing at the front door. As Stephen was going to be tested, I thought it best to be honest and up-front. The rain was pouring down on us, and as there was no shelter or porch, we looked a sight, like drowned rats begging to be let in.

I admit to feeling sorry for myself and questioned why my life was now so pitiful. Initially, the manager refused. Stephen had not met the requirements, and it had to be one rule for all. However, my pleas didn't fall on deaf ears. The manager felt compassion, especially after we had gone to Tenerife solely for this purpose. His eyes then darted to Stephen, beckoning with his thumb whilst saying in an authoritative tone: "Go on, get in there. How can you be messing your mother about like this?" My only emotion was relief that he had been taken off my hands, and I will always be grateful to this individual for simply having a heart.

It does what it says on the tin: Hope House gave my son his life back. He was a drug-free, 28-year-old man with the world at his feet. However, we had just received the devastating news that Scott had lost his life. How awful it must be for Julie that she no longer had her son.

She'd only just dealt with the trauma of his eye and now this! My heart ached as she was a young mum of 47 with many years of grieving ahead of her. I reiterated to Stephen how important it was to stay on the right path, so as not to endure the same fate.

Heroin is generally an age-out drug, but most habits have a lifespan of 12 years. By approximately 28, the energy for running and robbing to fund the addiction diminishes. Ducking and diving, climbing over walls and dodging police, plus the mental strategy needed to score, becomes too much effort.

I believe addicts are highly intelligent people, and if their intellect was channelled into a business or enterprise, rather than scoring, they could be entrepreneurs. Never underestimate them. Beneath the surface of their addiction, they are human beings with as many capabilities as the next person. If treatment intervention has not occurred, they tend to replace the heroin with an alternative, and in most cases it's alcohol. Booze is cheaper, easier to lift off the shelf, and socially accepted. You can, therefore, be part of a circle rather than living a solitary existence which is what heroin is. Refraining from drinking is much harder to accomplish than abstaining from drugs. It can also be life-threatening to go cold turkey if alcohol dependent.

Concealing alcoholism is easier masked as drinkers can hold down a job even for years unnoticed. An alcoholic often is not just a down-and-out, living on a park bench, hugging their bottle. The true definition is someone who cannot live without a drink, regardless of their surrounding circumstances. Like Brian's brother, Melville, who upheld the professional role of headmaster, but was actually a blind drunk. He would have a bottle of spirits lodged between the books on the shelf in his office, taking regular swigs throughout the day.

After driving home intoxicated he would continue consuming and be verbally aggressive to his wife. As soon as he retired, he suffered a stroke, and his large pension was then used to pay the monthly fees of a convalescent home. He isolated himself from the other residents as he never deemed them as having anything intelligent to say. Instead, he amused himself by sitting alone in his room, clutching a framed photograph of his mother.

His wife, long-suffering Harriet, who was also in teaching, had nursed him at home for a few years before his confinement. She felt liberated when he was no longer in the house, even speaking openly of her hidden abuse. They had five children together, and she had worked full time whilst raising them. She breast-fed each one and spent hours preparing and cooking all her meals from fresh. I admired how she did it all and with such organisation and precision. Tragically, freedom didn't last long. She was diagnosed with secondary ovarian cancer that originated in the breast. She refused further chemotherapy, as it made her feel so ill, and died six months later aged 66.

A heroin addict, however, becomes physically ill early on, and their appearance speaks a thousand words; so, they cannot maintain it. It's common to first start using in the late teens, which is the mental age they remain throughout the habit as they cannot "grow." The drug numbs all emotions, preventing the learning process of loss and life's issues such as relationships. It's only after experiencing these situations that we gather maturity, enabling us to deal with the next phase. This is why it was impossible to make Stephen see sense.

Whilst at rehab, he was taught domestic skills such as cooking, cleaning and shopping, which all the patients shared on a rota basis. Previously I had done everything for him, which he'd taken for granted.

Coming back to Swindon after rehab was not an option. He would fail. So, Stephen enrolled in a dry house in Weymouth once he completed treatment. He spent most days at the beach, but after a period, it wasn't enough to stimulate his mind. A friend suggested he transfer to Bournemouth as the N/A meetings were more accessible and frequent. He was there less than a few weeks when he met his first serious girlfriend, Nicky, in a nightclub, where he only consumed soft drinks. I went up for a visit, only to be told by a co-habitant at the dry house that he was out with his girlfriend.

Girlfriend?? I was shocked. He was supposed to be concentrating on his recovery, not girls. Stephen later rolled up with her and her young children, aged eight and five, strapped in the back of the car. I was horrified. He couldn't even look after himself, let alone two small children. Nothing I said made any difference, and he moved in with her a few weeks later. She was two years younger than him, a shoulder-length brunette with a pretty face, which was always in full make-up. Her green eyes were her most attractive feature, but she did struggle with her weight, which leaned towards the chubby side.

As he became more involved with Nicky, the attendance of the meetings fizzled. Stephen was so over the moon to have finally found a girlfriend and somebody who loved him that he let his recovery programme go out of the window. Professionals recommend you do not enter into a relationship until you're at least a year clean as you need to utilise this time to concentrate on just yourself.

Although he looked attractive, Stephen struggled to get a woman. Due to shyness, he couldn't hold a sensible conversation. After the honeymoon period, Nicky's true persona came to light. She was a very expensive lady, making demands which he could not fulfil. He didn't fall back into the drugs trap but swapped his addiction to his old gambling demon, which she encouraged to pay for the finer things she wanted. She socialised often and was a bit of a party girl. I felt a church girl would have been more suited.

I was actually surprised how well he coped with her children, and they did love him. Stephen did complain to me that their tantrums and whinging got on his nerves sometimes, but he remained patient and never raised his voice. I was glad he experienced true love as some people search a lifetime and never find it, but I knew that it was happening at the wrong time. Nevertheless, I did accept her, and she became a frequent visitor to my home. I even helped her out financially a couple of times to pay heating bills she couldn't afford. Following a string of turbulent rows, the relationship came to an end after 18 months, and she kicked him out.

An assessment by a Consultant Psychiatrist, 12 months before meeting Nicky, diagnosed Stephen as needing psychological therapy for a whole year, given the chronic nature of his symptoms and how entrenched they were. This disorder was independent from his drug, gambling and sex addictions. He had a number of borderline traits for someone having personality difficulties, including low self-esteem, presumably relating to his bullying at school and college. He was suffering with voices in his head, panic attacks when on buses or in crowds, and paranoia.

Stephen commenced sessions with a female key worker but began having sexual fantasies about her, which he openly divulged, and she ceased treating him. He never bothered to continue with the alternative male colleague, as he was trying to live like a normal-minded person. This was impossible. The reason the relationship with Nicky broke down was that she didn't understand his needs. She would mimic me in the background during my telephone conversations with him, as I would be reeling off a list of things he had to do. She thought I babied him and found it irritating as this was her boyfriend, an adult, not realising what I was saying was imperative. As her own brother used heroin on-and-off but was capable of being independent, she couldn't comprehend why Stephen could not.

Back on the accommodation trail, as Stephen wanted to remain in Bournemouth, we spent the day searching for a place. He was on housing benefit; so, his options were very limited as the majority of landlords discriminated against you. A letting agency accepted him for a bedsit at 50 Francis Road, providing I paid a £500 deposit and the first three months' rent up front. It was a quiet area opposite a bowling green, and we made it homey with furnishings from the charity shop.

Things appeared to be looking up, but expense and upheaval were waiting around the corner. I was wiping the loo with toilet wipes then proceeded to flush them, which regrettably blocked the cistern. As each bedsit in the building ran off this cistern, the plumber quoted parts and labour at £600. Unknowingly, my innocent actions had just cost me a small fortune!

Wayne, who Stephen knew from the meetings, asked if Stephen wanted to join him on a trip to Thailand, as he went often to see his Thai girlfriend. Stephen begged me for the money to go, pleading that this would get Nicky out of his system, and he could start afresh when he got back. He flew out in May 2009, for a trip that would carve his destiny. I later found out the whole holiday was spent using prostitutes, which reignited a sex addiction that laid dormant since he was a teenager.

At 15 years old, he lumbered me with a phone bill of £340. I contacted the provider, sure they had made a mistake, but they confirmed the calls related to sex lines. He denied it and blamed it on his dad, so I put a block on all those numbers. It didn't stop him. He began stealing porn magazines from the newsagents. I didn't take it seriously due to his young age, and the problem never resurfaced until his late 20s. In Thailand he reintroduced alcohol to his body, which paved the way for his multiple addictions to go haywire. It was the same for a guy at rehab who kicked a crack addiction but relapsed after swigging back half a can of Stella.

CHAPTER ELEVEN

As promised, when Stephen returned, he did manage to find himself a job driving a school mini bus. When asked if he had any convictions for drink driving he truthfully replied no; drugs weren't even mentioned. The manager was happy with his work, but when the CRB check reared six weeks later highlighting his police record, it was instant dismissal. The manager was sorry to let him go, but this is a case of where your past comes back to haunt you. Not too downhearted, a job delivering furniture swiftly followed, but again he would cut corners. Instead of taking the old furniture back to the depot, he was caught dumping it in the woods. He was sacked once again.

Sex and gambling were ruling Stephen's mind. He was travelling miles around the southwest to casinos in the blue Corsa I had bought him. The petrol gauge was always on empty as he was red hot on his cash and what he would spend it on. He lived on the edge and was prone to being a bit of a bad boy, unlike the girls, who were the opposite. I only bought the car as transport for work, which turned out to be another lie. He pretended to be labouring with Wayne installing heating and plumbing equipment and said that he needed it to get to the sites.

Sometimes he would win at gambling, sometimes he would lose. He became an expert on knowing which fruit machines paid out on which days and times, which was now his full-time occupation. When he got lucky, he spent his winnings in the local brothels, as much as £800 in one week. He was also spending his £60 a week housing benefit, which I then had to replace. In reality, he owed me £50,000 over the 12 years, meaning I was short for my retirement.

Even though I had finished working nights four years before, my sleeping pattern had never recovered. I still struggled to get even a few hours due to the anxiety of my son. We were getting too old to deal with this, being in our 60s. Something wasn't right. A mother always knows. I hadn't heard from Stephen for four days, Thursday through to Monday. Had he even attended the plumbing and heating course I managed to get for him by the skin of my teeth? Reaching his early 30s now, it was time for him to get on and find some stability; so, I thought this would be an ideal start.

My gut feeling was reinforced when Kevin came to see me on the Sunday evening. He had just returned from Bournemouth without making contact as Stephen wasn't answering the door or his mobile phone. The curtains were drawn and the Corsa was parked outside, and Kevin waited around in case he had gone out on foot. Kevin was desperate to get back the drugs Stephen was holding for him, which were worth £300 but had a street value of £900. It's common for dealers to pay people to hold their stash as they themselves are known to police and likely to be searched.

As their paths had crossed recently, Stephen saw an opportunity to make some easy money to return to Thailand. I refused to fund a second trip, despite his blackmail threats of "I will take one big hit and get rid of myself," as I didn't take it seriously. It was also ironic that Stephen, being much less influential than Kevin, had managed to get Kevin hooked on gambling too! They were partners in crime, planning which days they would go to "The Gala" without stepping on the other's toes. They fell out at times because Stephen would go the day before Kevin's turn and clear out the fruit machines. He knew they would be full, taking away Kevin's chance of winning.

The Gala was the in-place for bingo. I even got dragged along a few nights, but never won anything. I felt the environment damaging to the mind due to the flashing lights, loud noise and intensity in people's presence. It gave me a headache; so, it must have made Stephen's head rocket, even feeling claustrophobic by the time we left.

On Monday morning I phoned Sarah, relaying my fears that he could be dead. She dismissed me as being ridiculous, but I did call

999 anyway to establish his whereabouts. An officer was sent to the premises, and we had to just sit and wait.

A telephone call confirmed what I had feared. Stephen was dead from what appeared to be a heroin overdose. He was found on the edge of the bed, slumped over, wearing just his dressing gown. His body had decomposed quicker than usual due to the heating being left on full blast. The condition indicated he had passed away four days prior, all alone in his bedsit.

Sadness and anger were the two emotions running through me, and I burst into tears. Sad because he had lost his young life, and I was never going to see him again. Anger because it needn't have come to this, if only he had done the right thing. The five remaining members of the family gathered in my living room, numb with shock and unable to digest the news.

It was bizarre that on this very day, the postman delivered Stephen's ticket for Thailand. He was due to return for a second time to enjoy the Christmas and New Year festivities. He talked me into paying for another holiday, again on the basis he would get himself right.

When holding the ticket in my hand, I made an instant decision to treat my three girls to a fortnight trip to the country, which was received as uplifting. It was partly to make up for neglecting them during Stephen's addiction and also as a pilgrimage to feel closer to him.

I had promised to let Kevin know about Stephen, and I robotically dialled his number, saying two words—"he's dead"—and then hung up.

Within two hours, Vinnie, Kevin's cousin, was at the door. His body language was cold, and without offering any condolences, he went on to say: "I am not having Kevin blamed for this. Blood is thicker than water." From the way he was acting, you wouldn't think he had just lost his close friend. He was fishing for information as Kevin must have been panicking that a bad batch he had supplied could have been responsible. Vinnie mentioned a camera positioned at the side of the main entrance to the bedsits, which would confirm whether Kevin had been on video.

Vinnie was an only child, born to older parents who had both died from cancer by the time he was 11. For the remainder of this childhood, he was raised by Kevin's mother, who was the sister of his mum. All three of them resided together in an end terrace house just opposite the bus stop. The grief of being an orphan overwhelmed him. He once slapped a girl hard across the face for taunting him about having no mother or father.

He joined the childhood gang later than the others but had an underlying jealousy of Stephen, who had loving parents, something he craved. Jealousy makes people very ugly, and Vinnie began abusing Stephen with punches if he failed to obey. Before clenching his fist, he would ask where Stephen wanted it, the stomach or the face.

It must run in the family, as Vinnie was also a pasty looking child but introduced fake tan to his skin by adulthood. He had also beefed out due to working out at the gym. He sprouted into a conventionally handsome guy, spiking his strawberry blonde hair, and became a female magnet. He even tried his luck with Julie, a yummy mummy, who wasn't that much older as she'd been a teenage mum. Being wrinkle-free with shoulder-length blonde hair and piercing blue eyes, what guy wouldn't? He insinuated: "Cor she's a bit of alright for an older woman."

He classed myself and Brian as surrogate parents, and was a regular visitor to our home over the years. Even to the present day, I would lend him money, as I felt sorry for him, which he duly paid back. Ironically, if anyone borrowed from him, it had to be paid back plus interest, which was doubled if exceeding the deadline.

Due to his family circumstances, the council awarded Vinnie his own flat when he reached 18. It was on storey nine of a high-rise building. He made it homey with the help of Scott and his carpentry skills. Scott fitted new wooden doors throughout and installed a modern kitchen, scoring drugs with the money he had earned. Vinnie later purchased the place, securing a mortgage based on his full-time job at a warehouse. Shortly after, Vinnie began dating Gemma, who fell pregnant early into the relationship. Following the birth of their daughter, things turned sour, and she went her own way. Vinnie took full custody and provided the child with stability, and a very loving home.

Despite his behaviour toward Stephen during adolescence, they remained friends with divided beliefs. Vinnie lost patience with Stephen's lifestyle, having no understanding of why he couldn't pull himself together and get a job. Recovery was a waste of time in his eyes, although essential for long-term abstinence, referring to it as wishy-washy praying. Stephen felt more comfortable around Kevin, who never pressured him because Kevin was in the same boat himself and mirrored his plight.

Narrow-minded Vinnie failed to recognise he was an addict himself. He smoked cannabis every evening, which made him paranoid and moody. There was a regular odour of the residue in his flat. Vinnie had a stereotype of an addict in his head, and because he owned his own home and held down a job, he didn't fit the criteria of being one. It was recreational.

The day after the police discovered Stephen had died, we all travelled up to Bournemouth by bus to clear out his belongings. We packed his things up and loaded them into the little blue Corsa, which we came home in. It felt like we were bringing part of him back with us. On arriving home, I was disturbed by a knock at the door. Upon answering it, I was faced with a very shell-shocked Alfie.

He had been told about the death but could not truly believe it until he had heard it from the horse's mouth. It sheds light on how these addicts do not fully comprehend they are dicing with death. Every time you take a hit, you are playing a game of Russian roulette. I was civil to Alfie, although a little surprised he had shown his face as he gave Stephen one hell of a beating once for ripping him off with some gear.

Was all I had been through to any avail, as I'm twelve years on and no further forward from day one? I had endured more heartache, pain and stress imaginable from fighting this losing battle. The £50,000 it cost was of great detriment to my finances, as we were not rich people. It was just subsidised through saving plans and my wages. I would do it all over again if it meant keeping him alive, as a mother never gives up in her heart, and my love for him is unconditional. Call it habit or unacceptance, but I was still pricing up rehabs after his death. This was to satisfy my knowing as to whether there was something more I could have done to save him.

DI Cartwright, the policeman assigned to the case, was responsible for establishing whether it was an overdose, or if foul play was involved. The morning Stephen's body was found, I had a telephone conversation with Cartwright, and to be quite frank, I didn't like his attitude. He had no compassion and made no secret he was dealing with just another "drug death statistic." He wanted to get the job done and wrapped up as soon as possible, but for me I needed answers and to be sure Kevin's drugs were found. During the initial routine search, his officers didn't find anything, but after carrying out a second check himself, based on my information, he discovered them. He was embarrassed as he had located them easily by simply opening the top draw of the dressing table. "Even a five-year-old could have spotted them!' were his exact words.

His PCs got a severe telling off for sloppy policing, and it also made his persona soften towards me. Fingerprints confirmed Kevin was connected to the drugs, but there were no clues from the camera as it was a dummy. Cartwright tried to make light of the tragic situation by saying he had stumbled across Stephen's large pile of adult porn mags. The family were now building up a rapport with him, which made him feel comfortable to say something so sensitive.

At this stage, I was unsure of the cause of death and dubious because Stephen had been hanging around with some unsavoury characters. All the occupants in the building were questioned, and the gentleman upstairs confirmed that recently many unfamiliar faces would come and go. Stephen did mention a few weeks before, when staying with me for ten days, that an acquaintance had free run of his bedsit. He was using the place to hide his gun and drugs in exchange for cash, and he had the one and only set of keys. Stephen had no personal interest in using, so I suppose you could call it "dirty cash."

I wasn't happy to accept that it was either an accidental overdose or suicide, so DI Cartwright reluctantly agreed to meet and hear our suspicions. "If you can't get to Bournemouth by 4:30 pm I am going home." Would he be this blasé if it was his son lying in the morgue?

After greeting us at reception with his hands in his pockets, we all then trailed through the corridors to his office. He was a very tall fellow, verging over 6 ft., with dark, spiky hair. His approximate age was late-40s, and he wore a dark suit with his shirt open without a tie. He was a charismatic character who would remark "yeah, yeah" in a friendly tone when suggestions were made.

As the initial meeting was informative, it put me at ease. People in authority often made me feel belittled. It was probably because I didn't have status, so I never felt important against someone with it. His mannerisms weren't those of a high-ranking detective, but he was taking it seriously and arranged for the DCI to listen to our concerns. An interesting point he made is that only two sets of people use two mobile phones. One are the police, and the other are dealers.

Both officers ruled out any other persons entering the property, as Stephen held the only set of keys. They could not be cut by a general locksmith due to their "special making." I proceeded to stun them by stating that I had found a shop able to do so. Anything can be done on the black market. The letting agent gave me a set temporarily to clear out Stephen's possessions, which is when I did my own detective work. My gut instinct that someone else was involved could not be proved; so, I had to lay it to rest. It's a mother's prerogative to look at every angle as you need to know what happened to your child.

The post mortem determined heroin had been injected into his big toe. So, the two conclusions were suicide or accidental overdose. Stephen was clean for three years, so perhaps his tolerance level was low and his body unable to withstand the hit. Or maybe he had just had enough. The coroner's officer said that only Stephen knows the truth, and he has taken it to his grave.

The coroner's officer was a jolly man in his 60s, with the patience of a saint with relation to the numerous telephone calls I made to him. "Mrs. Cowell," in an exaggerated tone, was the words he used to start all of his sentences when answering the repeated questions I put to him. Graphic conversations flowed between us regarding the process of performing a post mortem, as I wanted to know everything. He even divulged to me on one occasion that he had dissected a female and stood with her private parts in the palm of his hands. This wasn't regular procedure, which is why he recollected the one of a few isolated examinations of that area.

Nothing is free, and the funeral directors charged £80 to transport Stephen's body back from Bournemouth to Swindon. Due to the decomposition, we were advised against seeing him as he was unrecognisable. I wouldn't be robbed of never touching him again; so, we felt him whilst covered head-to-toe in a body bag. When buried, I wanted him dressed in his grey shorts, as he loved them, wearing them endlessly around the house with his white T-shirt. Ironically, he was one of five males in the chapel of rest, ranging from 18 to 73, and all were suicides.

CHAPTER TWELVE

The hearse was driven through the streets of Park North, passing Stephen's regular haunts. He knew the estate like the back of his hand. It was his home.

Propped up at the front of the coffin was a pillow-shaped wreath, which his sisters had bought. It was made up of red and white flowers, matching the colours of the Liverpool Football team, who Stephen had supported since he was a boy. It was also a symbol for his love of sleeping in bed. The funeral service was held at his old Sunday school and was packed out.

Stephen only ever went to Sunday school to receive the two chewitt sweets handed out at the end from the round tartan tin. The Elder would pick up my kids in his estate car at 11 am, and I would use the time to get the roast cooked in peace. They loved going in his car as it was novel for them. He also collected a few others along the way; but, sadly, they weren't all clean and would smell. Stephen was finicky, so would aim to sit as far from them as possible.

The memorial was beautiful, dedicated solely to him and not so much about religious speeches. We did sing "All things bright and beautiful," which I felt was very fitting. He was unique, and although troubled, Stephen still brought smiles with his jokes and sense of humour. Independent of his shyness, he was a poser, despite not having two pennies to rub together. Quite often, he drove around wearing sunglasses, with his tanned arm hanging out the window looking the part.

Death travels wide and far, bringing people out of the woodwork whom I hadn't seen for years. Paddy came to pay his respects and was the first of the congregation to snigger about Stephen being a compulsive liar. Paddy knew him to a tee and had been subjected to his lies many times. Paddy touched me with his comment: "God, I can't believe the turnout. At other addicts' funerals, there were just one or two people ."

To compliment Stephen further, they all pulled out their glad rags and wore shirts and ties, rather than the normal attire of hoodies. Instead of flowers, we requested donations, which reached £119 and was later passed on to a local rehab. The money was then used to fund days out for recovering addicts.

I buried Stephen at the same resting place as Scott, as they were friends and should be together. Julie, who had visited me days after Stephen's death, said that on the Thursday he supposedly died, she had driven drove past my house, not knowing what had happened. The feeling that overwhelmed her about Stephen was the same feeling described as someone walking over your grave.

Out of the blue, DI Cartwright called, saying he was now in a position to return Stephen's mobile phone. It was confiscated as part of the investigation, as it held dealer contacts, which was useful to the police. Cartwright was impressed with our supportive family unit. To emphasise my care, he even commented on the uneaten packed lunch of cheese sandwiches and banana I'd made, which he found when searching the Corsa.

As a personal favour, Cartwright established Stephen's last movements for closure to the family. My mind was racing with questions as to why he died, and I will always be grateful to Cartwright for going that extra mile. The night before Stephen's death, CCTV at the casino was out of action, but the staff recall him losing £1100. Maybe this was the final straw that pushed him over the edge?

I'm flapping! The phone would be personally delivered instead of being mailed in a jiffy bag. A detective inspector coming down, specially to see us! We had a cup of tea at the house before venturing to a country pub for lunch, my treat. Half of us travelled in the Corsa and the other half in his four-by-four. The sun was shining, so we sat outside chatting about general life. It was the time Prime Minister Gordon Brown was branded a squatter for his slow reaction to vacate

No 10 after losing the election. It was splashed across the front page of *The Sun*, which Cartwright found hilarious, seeing it that morning when getting petrol. He was real.

We saw Cartwright one final time for the inquest a few months later. It had to be held in Bournemouth, the town in which Stephen died. The cause of death was recorded as "heroin toxicity," and the verdict being: "The deceased died as a consequence of the abuse of drugs." The wording used to describe Stephen's appearance on the accompanying pathology report was an "overweight male," which would have horrified him. He had bulked out prior to his death due to his gym visits coupled with the use of steroids. His diet had also changed to increase his protein intake, and he was eating whole chickens or a box of half a dozen eggs in one serving. He was eating me out of house and home and costing me a fortune, but I preferred this to the opposite.

Even this day wasn't hassle-free as Sarah managed to get a speeding ticket on the way in the blue Corsa. She drove at 40 mph, which was within the limit, but it suddenly reduced to 30 mph at the top of the hill. Regrettably, there wasn't time to adjust to the change, and she got clicked. The penalty arrived a week later with a fine of £60, or three licence points if a speed awareness course was attended. She was two minutes late for the course, so they wouldn't allow her in, and the fine was reinstated.

The car was a curse as one thing after another was going wrong, and I was forever paying out. I shouldn't have kept it, really, as we never drove, and Sarah used it as a run-around. Perhaps seeing it reminded me of him, but it was time for it to go, and I lined up a sale for £300. Lo and behold, a few days prior the head gasket blew due to the water not being filled up. I can't blame Sarah, as the warning light never displayed on the dash, and she didn't know anything about maintaining a car.

I took it to the garage at the end of the road and was told it would cost £500 to fix. There was no point as I was only due £300 back on it; so, he offered to take it off my hands for £50 scrap. I later learned the mechanic repaired it himself and sold the car on for £500. The part itself costs next to nothing. It's the labour involved making it so expensive. As he did the work himself, he had made the easiest buck ever. That's business, I suppose, but I would never stoop this low, especially not to a bereaved mother.

Heartbroken and wanting to get away from it all, I booked a cruise with Brian, our first holiday since Stephen's death, four months previous. After years, I could now go away without worrying as to what was he was getting up to at home. We had a lovely two-week sail around the Mediterranean and were unprepared for what was facing us when we got back.

Our French patio doors were all boarded up. I couldn't quite register what I was seeing.

I knew Michelle was checking on the house, so I phoned her immediately to ask: "What the bloody hell's going on?" I had been burgled, something I had never experienced before. Little was taken. It was more the inconvenience they had left behind. Replacement glass in the door and a new window frame was needed, as it was damaged when wrenching it open. That little episode cost me £600 as it wasn't worth claiming on the insurance. The uncanny part is that every room was ransacked except Stephen's bedroom, which was left untouched.

In my heart, I knew Kevin was responsible, probably trying to retrieve the £300 drug money he lost. I think his target was the white vanity case he remembered from all those years ago, but unlucky for him, I no longer kept it. All that was taken was some cosmetic jewellery (dress rings) which were diamond encrusted, but of course only fakes. Upon first inspection they would appear real. You think you are stealing a fortune, but, in reality, they were worth £20. I had taken my original jewellery with me, so for once I got one up on the bad guy.

Trying to catch a thief is not top priority for the police, and I had to chase them regularly for an update. The information they came back with is that fingerprints were found belonging to my son. I got the impression they were implying he was responsible, but they got egg on their face when told bluntly he was already dead!

A year later when visiting his grave, speaking as though he could hear us, I expressed my anger that he was underneath the ground. This particular day, a pack of playing cards were placed on the headstone, and I knew instantly it was Kevin, recognising them as being gambling buddies. Although from the day Stephen died, Kevin's mother told me that he no longer played, being so cut up.

Maybe their friendship did mean something because, although we didn't understand them, they seemed to understand each other. The photograph of Stephen that Kevin requested had since been enlarged and placed in his living room. Also, not being able to drive himself, he had taken advantage of the opportunity of being chauffeured around by Stephen, and that was partly a loss to him too.

Shortly after Stephen's death, I had asked Kevin to come to the house to give any information about Stephen's final days. This was to determine his state of mind. Was he depressed? Kevin duly turned up and was co-operative, but he insisted we speak outside for fear of being tape recorded. He was a small-time dealer and watched his back, fully aware the police had confiscated his gear from the bedsit.

He was still cohabitating in a council flat with the same girl, Leanne, whom he had been with since they were teenagers. She was from a well-to-do family who took an instant disapproval to Kevin, fearing he was a bad influence. Her parents gave her an ultimatum: him or them. She chose him, and never saw them again. She always had a bitchy nature but had to change her lifestyle in order to mix with the rough and ready. Kevin never allowed her to touch the really hard stuff, but she smoked weed regularly.

They had a daughter, now aged twelve, and had recently added to the family with a set of girl twins. Could Kevin ever contemplate dropping them on their heads like he threatened my granddaughters? I often wondered how they raised children under these chaotic conditions, but I think the praise lies mainly with his mother. She was the maternal driving force that held it all together, as they lived with her for years after their first baby. Despite the fact he lived the lifestyle of a would-be gangster, every year he played the family man and took Leanne and the kids for a week's caravan holiday in Weymouth.

Stephen got on with Leanne, who even offered him some empathy for the scale of driving he did going from casino to casino. She commented: "God, you must be tired doing all that," and allowed him to join them on one occasion to the coast. When returning, Stephen expressed how much Kevin enjoyed himself, mucking in making sand castles as "Leanne babe," the name he always called her, only allowed him out once a week without her. Although to his credit he never protested, Kevin must have relished the freedom of the sea air.

Now in his mid-30s, never having been employed, through choice, Kevin's looks had taken a battering. He appeared far older than his years. Still pasty-faced, he now wore a woolly hat wherever he went, to hide his receding hair line. Drugs were still being injected into his body, but the abuse was catching up with him as he now suffers a heart defect.

CHAPTER THIRTEEN

I contacted Wayne to say we were jetting out to Thailand in April 2011, for a fortnight. Coincidentally, he would be in the country at the same time, and we agreed to meet up. He did me a favour by bringing Stephen's bike to Swindon when he travelled down in his car for the funeral. I don't forget things like that as he helped me out at a time when I needed it. He was an average looking guy with blonde hair, verging around 6 feet tall and blessed with the gift of the gab. His personality made him appear more attractive than he was, as his face was flawed with scars from acne, also looking older than his years. He came from a fairly wealthy family, one of two boys. His parents owned a boat which they used actively in the summer.

His ten-year habit had put them through hell. Wayne was now clean to a point but still indulged in the odd joint of marijuana and a beer. He was also unable to stay faithful due to his sex addiction bubbling under the surface. It's not actually about the sex itself. It's just another way of getting that adrenaline rush, which is the same hit regardless of what your addiction is.

Myself and the three girls arrived at Bangkok after an 11-hour flight for a transfer to Pattaya, all knackered but excited. I was nervous going through this airport due its stigma, but to my surprise, it was modern, and we were processed quickly. The Four Seasons Hotel was lovely, exuding an oriental feel and essence. Soft Asian music played in the background, and the staff wore traditional Thai clothing. You were greeted with a bow of the head in conjunction with clasped hands, resembling a praying stance.

The swimming pool was a circle, and the rooms were built around it from ground to four floors up. Pattaya was a busy place, and we used the tuc-tucs, a form of taxi, to get around, which were driven at speed. A truck style vehicle with an open air back and a bench each side, seating eight. A blatant sewerage aroma was off putting and circulated the whole town, so could not be evaded.

The mainland beach was not the paradise you envisage, for tropical beauty. It was a 20-minute boat trip. Koh Lan was beautiful; the clear crystal water coupled with pure white sand mirrored a scene from the Bounty advert. A familiar site was older men hand-in-hand with very young Thai girls, all being tiny framed and fragile. One slender American woman commented that when standing next to them she felt like the Amazon. This is the sex capital of the world, although some go specifically to find a wife. A Yank with a southern drawl was frolicking in the sea with a lady of the night of similar age to him. He showered her with affection, which she welcomed, absorbing his words of "I just want to take you home with me." The majority of men were Russian, but Australian nationals could also be overheard.

We ventured down the infamous "Walking Street" where Stephen had spent most of his holiday. It is a long area packed with multiple bars and clubs advertising sexual services, even handing out menus of what they offer. The working girls congregated at the front of the premises whilst others sat at the bar touting for business, some looking well-weathered. The late nights and poor nutrition had taken its toll, poverty being the underlying factor. It cost 300 baht (£6) to hire a prostitute for a week, plus her expenses such as meals. Half the money goes to the bar, and the woman receives the other half. She would then send this back to her family in the villages, whose only other source of income is selling rice. Prostitution is widely accepted, although you had to work for an establishment as it is illegal to go solo on the street. Business had been hurt by the ongoing recession; hence, the amount of females standing idle.

The lady boys perform a show at Alcazar theatre, and we booked tickets to watch them entertain. They all dance in sequence to the choreography whilst miming the songs played out. I really could not believe they were once men as they were so feminine, even prettier than the women. They had skin like porcelain, and it was easy to understand how a man could be fooled into thinking he had picked up a female. They are such a prominent part of the Thai culture and something I would not want to have missed.

Like Stephen, we are all a bit fussy and struggled with the food. We ordered steak, only to be enlightened by Wayne that it's actually buffalo, a cheap imitation which tasted awful. To receive the real McCoy, you had to be prepared to pay around £30. We joined Wayne and his girlfriend, Poi, for dinner and reminisced about Stephen, who would only eat at a little cafe called Maggie's. She was an English lady who took pity on him and cooked exactly what he wanted, as she got most of her food imported.

A fellow guest, hearing our plight, recommended a restaurant called Mantras which catered to all cuisines. The guy had told me about the place whilst I was using the pool and struck up a conversation with him. He was a healthy early-60s British male who had clearly benefited from the finer things in life.

He was a retired aviation engineer who travelled business class, which included being collected from his front door. He actively used the golf courses, which was the main purpose for his holiday, amongst other things, I later learned. I'm not tactful and voiced my opinion of "bloody disgusting" when he asked what I thought of the sex industry in Thailand. The exploiting of vulnerability for one's own gratification was something I was very averse to. He must have been trying to gauge my reaction. I felt he was looking for confirmation that it was OK. But deep down, he knew it was wrong as he was sheepish when I spotted him with a call girl young enough to be his granddaughter.

Also staying at the Four Seasons was a friendly guy in his mid-40s from Atlanta, Georgia, a civilian working for the American Army in Iraq as a mechanic. He had leave and wanted to holiday in a civilized country that wasn't too far away. Not being used to hotels, he was raiding the mini bar in his room, thinking they were complimentary, only to be hit with a bill he couldn't pay. He called his sister back home in the US, who was livid but covered the cost, enabling him to continue spending.

He would pay extra and bring a different girl to breakfast each morning after she had serviced him all night. I thought more highly of him for treating her as a human with some dignity, rather than just kicking her out in the morning as an object. There seemed to be some genuine affection between him and one particular girl, as I saw her out of the corner of my eye playfully attempting to poke him with her cutlery.

Bangkok, the city that never sleeps, is where we were staying for two nights, to seize the opportunity. When looking over the wall on the top floor of the hotel, you get a bird's eye view, and the sight is breathtaking. When strolling around the bustling streets, I jumped out of my skin after observing a giant rat. It ran straight past my feet and into the drain below the high pavements, made to accommodate the rainy season.

A speed boat took us down the harbour river, as it's the best way to appreciate the temples and architecture. Along the embankment were Buddhas carved out of marble with jewelled faces; the detail was outstanding. When docking, we passed an elderly vagrant who was sitting in his house, a netted tent, accommodating all his wares. He was very resourceful, possessing his own pots and pans, which he managed to use even through his bleak circumstances.

We struck up a conversation as he spoke very good English, coming from a prominent Thai family, and had clearly been well-educated. He had white mucus covering his face and the other parts of his body that were visible, presumably due to poor living conditions. I don't know how he ended up like this, but it proves anyone can go from the top to the bottom. We each gave him some money and wished him well, and in turn he said he would pray for us.

The notorious Bang Kwang prison dubbed The Bangkok Hilton was heavily associated with Thailand. We contacted the British Embassy in the hope of visiting a Western prisoner, as the majority are held for drug offences. I guess I wanted to see how drugs can ruin your life from every different angle. After faxing a photocopy of our passports through we were granted a visiting order.

The Embassy asked us to report if any foul play was witnessed, as they suspected it went on.

Carl Neeson was the only prisoner available that day, and his name instantly rang a bell. We recalled watching a TV documentary shortly after his arrest, highlighting the hardships of the jail. It was an hour before entering, as Thai visitation was priority. So, we walked across to the prison shop opposite. It was well known that the diet was rice and fish eggs, and we thought he would appreciate a change, buying him oranges and biscuits.

The building, spanning a large area, was long and flat, having a chilling feel, which made us all a bit apprehensive. Upon entry, you're frisked by the guards, all wearing khaki uniforms, then led to a line of kiosks in a courtyard. A shield of glass separates visitor and prisoner with a telephone on each side enabling both parties to communicate. It was impersonal, not allowing any physical touching.

Cries and shrieks echoed from a woman of African appearance, accompanied by two small children, when observing the physical state of her partner. The marks on his face indicated he had been viciously beaten, but due to the language barrier, I couldn't understand what she was saying. However, her anger seemed to be directed at the guards, and I felt nervous for her safety. She did manage to calm down and continue her visit without bringing further attention to herself.

Carl appeared red-faced and watery-eyed, a young man aged 29 of slim build wearing a baseball cap, T-shirt and football shorts. When speaking, his broad Cornish accent was immediately apparent, despite having spent the last nine years locked up. It was a very surreal moment, and I was overwhelmed with emotion.

Only five minutes before arriving was he told of our visit, despite the staff knowing for a week. This was them being manipulative, a cruel tactic. We were his first visitors in three years, his father being the last one. Quite easily, this could have been Stephen as it's a crime I could envisage him committing. I don't know what's worse, languishing for 23 years in a Thai hell hole or being six feet under.

Carl was not a hardened criminal, just an immature 19-year-old trying to make money selling ecstasy tablets. He was heading for the bars in the city but was arrested at the airport after a UK tip-off. It was his second time to the country after first holidaying as an 18th birthday present from his parents. The destination was recommended by the travel agent, and after staying seven nights, it gave him the notion to return and deal. He was co-operative in answering our questions and remained upbeat when we each spoke to him individually.

He learned fluent Thai, regardless of having learning difficulties, and earned himself a job in the prison hospital. He was responsible for clinical tasks and dispensing medicines, which is ironic considering he's banged up for drug trafficking! The two Thai doctors he worked alongside were also prisoners and had been convicted of murdering their wives. One case being so gruesome as he'd chopped her up into little pieces and flushed her down the toilet.

For the first year, you are permanently shackled to prevent suicide, as this is when it's most likely, whilst adapting to your unimaginable surroundings. Carl attempted suicide by starvation and was placed in the medical unit as his weight plummeted. After viewing the guy in the next bed pass away, he realised he didn't actually want to die.

I walked away with sadness, but not bitterness, even though I had lost my own son to drugs. I respect that everyone has their own opinion, and some will feel that Carl got what he deserved. For me, however, I can only commend the way he has coped with his situation.

Six months after we returned home, Bangkok flooded with many of its buildings and sites destroyed. Life must be mapped out as had we not of gone at that time we wouldn't have seen what we did.

Two years later Michelle and Sarah traced Carl through the UK prison system, where he had been transferred for the remainder of his sentence. He accepted their request to meet, as they wanted to obtain his permission to mention him in the book, which he granted.

They travelled down by train to a jail in the South of England. Carl was in an open environment consisting of prisoners and family members, including children, and the atmosphere was chaotic. The room was scattered with tables moulded to the floor and three chairs attached to each one. The prisoner is confined to being seated throughout the whole visit, but they were not differentiated by their clothing. At first glance, he looked different from how they remembered, almost like he'd lost his mojo. However, he did appear pleased to see them, and the chocolate they purchased for him on the premises broke the ice.

He explained prison life in Thailand was outdoors, allowing him the enjoyment of playing football. This made being incarcerated bearable compared to the UK, despite having the perks of a phone and TV in his own cell. The food, of course, was more edible. He even commented that he had filled out, enhanced by his use of the gym.

Carl did stress that had he transferred earlier, he would already be free. After 3.5 hours they hugged before he returned to his cell, reciting his plans: "7:30 *Coronation Street* and 8 *EastEnders*." They laughed as here he was having done hardened time in one of the world's toughest jails, yet he was enlivened by life's simplicities.

CHAPTER FOURTEEN

My Spanish bank statement arrived showing for the third month in a row that no rent had been paid, leaving me anxious. It was a two-bedroom, ground-floor property in Torrevieja, near Alicante, with a shared communal pool. From the side view of my small garden sat the world-famous salt lake, which was used to heal ailments such as arthritis and as a beauty regime to cleanse your skin. You smear your body with the mud on the banks then wade into the lake to wash it off. Due to the salt in the water, you float, which is a very magical experience.

I was letting off my apartment on a long-term lease, the tenants arranged by Margi, the president who managed the residential estate. It was a verbal agreement as she was friends with the couple, knowing them from her home town in Wales. The renters, Steve and Teresa Payne, were in their late fifties. She was hippie-like, with long dark greying hair tied back in a ponytail, and she wore floor length patterned skirts. He was of a placid nature, with a history of chronic illness. The first six months they paid their rent in full, so a request to extend their tenancy was accepted.

After this period, payments for rent and bills became sporadic; then they just stopped. So, I was covering the cost myself. There wasn't a phone at the apartment; so, I had to call Margi's landline, and she would then walk around and ask them to come to her house. During our initial conversation, I was reassured a lump-sum from his UK pension was being paid early because of his health. Out of this money, I would be paid back everything they owed, which is all I ever wanted.

These excuses continued for many months, and our conversations became heated, although he never lost his cool. I believed his story and in giving people a chance, despite others having an adverse opinion. He owed me 7,500 euros, which included loss of rent and utilities. Do I evict him now and get nothing or wait a bit longer? After all, what's a few more months on top of what I have already lost? It's 500 euros each to get gas, electric and water reconnected, so cutting them off is not an easy decision.

After two years with no change, I flew out to Spain exasperated and stressed out. I should have taken the bull by the horns sooner, but I was grieving for my son and didn't have the strength to deal with this dilemma. I stayed with my friend who lived in a nearby town, someone I used to work with and had kept in touch. Her husband was 20 years her senior and currently battling secondary bowel cancer and undergoing chemotherapy. I was conscious not to cause any intrusion and was out most of the day.

It was time to come face-to-face with these people, knowing I had to be civil but really wanting to scream. I got a taxi to my apartment and met the Paynes at the garden gate. I didn't venture onto the property, which felt strange as I owned it. We had a lengthy talk under the hot Spanish sun, trying to protect myself as much as possible. I wore a sun hat and factor 50 lotion, plastering it on as I was wary of skin cancer. People would often joke that I looked like a snowman, but I didn't care. Again, I bought their lies that my money was imminent and felt content a resolution had been reached. I used the remainder of my time to have a bit of a holiday and enjoyed the beach. The Spanish recession was really kicking in at this point, and I saw my first homeless person sleeping on the beach.

I went to Patricia's Bar, one of a few around the estate, which was popular due to its karaoke nights, held outside. Regulars, ex-pats who lived here all year round, were really consumed with the place. One gentleman was dubbed "Leslie Presley" due to his Christian name being Leslie coupled with his love of Elvis. He was 84 years old and as fit as a fiddle, serenading customers with Elvis songs whilst dressed in a variety of costumes. He was the star of the show with his gold belts, wig and pointed boots, which he had especially made. His voice left a lot to be desired, but you could not deny he was an entertainer, performing all the moves, even the kicking out. In his mind, he believed he was Elvis, which I found endearing.

It was time to head back to the UK, in two minds as to whether I'd made any progress. Six weeks after being home, still no bloody money, I was absolutely furious. This time I was making another trip to Spain, accompanied by a man of German origin named Wagner, an old work colleague. He was 6ft 4in and built like a brick shithouse, with fair hair and blue eyes, a traditional Aryan look. He'd been married four times, producing eight children.

I had bumped into him recently, discovering he had an apartment close to ours. I explained our predicament, and because he was due to go out there, he wanted to help me reclaim my apartment. I flew out with him and his friend, accepting his kind invitation to stay at his place. I thought by bunking up with the two of them, it would save me the cost of a hotel. His friend was a lifer currently on parole for murder after serving 16 years in prison. I never asked any questions, although intrigued and uneasy, as I was with a convicted killer, but who am I to judge? Me a pensioner consorting with a murderer. It's been a colourful life with people always interested in my tales of woe.

Numerous visits to the Paynes in the baking heat, fobbed off with the same excuses, were taking their toll on my friendship with Wagner. He was so annoyed that I wouldn't just kick them out and cancel the direct debits for the bills. His mate also started to get shirty with me, and I certainly didn't want to upset him. In hindsight, perhaps, that is what I should have done. By my own admission I am a scatterbrain with a soft nature, and Wagner found my traits irritating. I may appear one way, but I am actually very switched on and underestimated.

Wagner's mild demeanour changed to that of an aggressive bully who was constantly shouting at me. The atmosphere among the three of us was divided, them on one side and me on the other. They were expressing their annoyance of me by exchanging derogatory looks. I awoke to find they had already gone out, locking me in the apartment, knowing I didn't have a key; so, I was housebound. Their anger had got so great they needed to dish out some kind of punishment.

The whole trip was a disaster, and I was no further forward. I was a 65-year-old woman, and the stress was not welcome at my age. When Michelle learned of the treatment I endured from Wagner, she was so incensed that she phoned him. Asking him if he enjoyed bullying an OAP, he brutally shouted: 'Fuck off, you cunt!"

I meant business, and three months later myself and Brian were in Spain to move into our apartment. Why should I pay out for accommodation when I have a property sitting there? My anger also extended to Margi as she put them in there yet failed to take responsibility, or even apologise. She would swan around with a manly physique whilst wearing her signature baseball cap, using the pool every afternoon. Her costume had one of those little skirts attached at the bottom, which always reminded me of a ballerina's tutu.

On each occasion, at Margi's house, I was met by her lethal son, Ricky, who Stephen had once gone nightclubbing with. An ex-heroin addict turned binge drinker with an intimidating personality, Margi herself was even scared of him. Mother and son shared a song, "Dirty Old Town" by The Pogues, on the karaoke box at Bar Patricia's, and were very good. It was done with ease, still with his fag between his fingers, and showed they had a bond.

He was a tall guy of solid build with a shaved head, although his natural colour was fair. In a rugged way he was sexy, but he let himself down as soon as he opened his mouth. Whenever he saw me coming he would growl: "Go home, will ya?" So I never ventured further than the gate. He didn't want to be mean and did have some compassion for my situation but was fed up with it.

Ricky was on police bail charged with assaulting his English girlfriend, who lived in the next town. They met whilst both residing in Spain and had a child, a little girl, now aged two. Due to the ongoing court case, all access to her was forbidden. It wasn't a one-off incident as I myself witnessed him attack his new girlfriend during a regular karaoke night. She pulled his seat back deliberately as he was just about to sit down. If he hadn't realised it, he would have gone straight on his arse. Because of her actions, he erupted and grabbed her up by the throat, knocking over all the chairs to the side of him. As soon as he kicked off, Margi dashed off so as not to endure any part of his violence. The barman added his two pence worth by saying: "You bring it on yourself, Candice." Before this incident happened, to support himself Ricky got a job at Bar Patricia's but was sacked for reasons unknown. He was then dependent on Margi to keep him, who was boosting her income by waiting tables at a local restaurant, Shelley's.

The squalid condition of the apartment left by the Paynes

Our key opened the door to the foulest odour I have ever smelt. Teresa was alone ironing, with the shutters down and windows closed. The place was in squalor; I didn't even recognise it. A small dog was rummaging around in the all the clothes strewn across the living room. In the front bedroom, boxes full of stuff were piled on top of one another from floor to ceiling, leaving no space to move. I was fuming and made no secret to hide it. So, even through her shock, she tried to pacify my anger. Steve arrived half an hour later with a concoction of medicines he had collected from the pharmacy.

Under Spanish law I wasn't allowed to kick them out; so, I told them we were moving in until they paid up. Legally this was permitted, and I was prepared to do so, even though the conditions made me feel sick. Brian put the kettle on as we were gasping, making it with tea-bags we bought with us. Teresa couldn't bear living with us, for even one night, and offered to go to friends for the evening.

After coming to this agreement, Brian and I popped out for a meal at 8:30 pm, returning at 10:30 pm to find them gone. Five minutes after we arrived home, they knocked at the door claiming to have nowhere to go. I had to be careful of squatter's rights, so I offered them to stay, but they refused. Luckily, a neighbour, Rosemarie, the black sheep of the estate, allowed them to sleep at hers, as news travels fast. She was a troublemaker, habitually breaking the estate's rules by parking her car in forbidden spaces. Her dog would bark at unsociable hours, due to its bed being in the garden, disturbing the peace.

With this knowledge I went to bed light-headed after knocking back a few large glasses of wine. At 1 am, I was awoken by the bell ringing and banging on the door, and as still a bit tipsy, I was unsure of my surroundings. I fumbled to the front door, opening it to see four uniformed police standing before me. The six patrol cars could be seen in the near distance with their blue lights flashing. The commotion had woken up the street and people were hanging out their doors. From the drama, anyone would think a murder had been committed. "Passport, Passport" is what they demanded in broken English, and I nervously hunted in my handbag.

Steve had reported me for unlawful eviction, egged on by Rosemarie. I had to present paperwork there and then to prove I was the owner, and once satisfied, they told me to report to the police station the next morning. I struggled to get back to sleep as the night's events were whirring around in my head. I laid there until I drifted off for a couple of hours around 6 am. It beggars belief that this couple had stayed in my apartment for two years rent-free, yet I was the one being hassled!

At the station, which was sat on a main road and directly opposite a large hypermarket, an interpreter was provided, allowing us to give our side of the story. She was a Russian lady in her 20s, who was very hostile and uninformative. We were at liberty to trust she was relaying our statement correctly, as she could have been saying anything for all I know.

After many hours in a secluded room, we were given the bad news that the case was going to court for prosecution. A small technicality in the Paynes' favour is that we didn't knock before entering the building. Further bad news followed, in that we could not remove their belongings until the case was heard, which could take up to four years. However, a preliminary hearing the same day decided that we were under no obligation to let them back in, and their belongings could be extracted.

For once, luck was on my side as it easily could have gone the other way. Margi opened up an empty apartment for the Paynes to stay in whilst all this kafuffle was going on. I warned her that the same thing would probably happen to the unaware proprietors, but Ricky soon piped up: "If he doesn't get out of there, I will break his fucking legs." You wouldn't want to mess with him! Steve's mother, who lived in Spain, collected their mass of stuff and took them in a few days later. We now had the daunting task of stripping the place down and refurbishing it.

I was aware that they still had keys; so, getting the locks changed was first on the agenda. They were both smokers, which left all the walls and ceilings brown. The cooker wires were ripped out, and all the other electrical appliances were broken.

From the evidence left behind, camera equipment and a case load of amateur videos, it appeared he had been making sex films to flog. I couldn't bear to keep the mattress they slept on; so, it was replaced. It took two weeks of solid cleaning and painting to restore the flat's original condition. I also had to spend a further 2,500 euros repairing the damage. The Paynes returned to Wales after the case was dropped. The property was now a bad omen, and I just wanted to sell up, already being 10,000 euros out of pocket.

CHAPTER FIFTEEN

L ife moseyed along, spending my days at the gym and seeing the family as time was my own, despite doing everything with a heavy heart. I gained some relief in not having the constant worry Stephen brought, as our health wouldn't have withstood much more. This wasn't how it was supposed to be. My expectations were for him to get his life sorted. My situation reflected Julie's in the fact that we had both lost a child, but there were differences. She was younger than I and had more time on this earth to suffer the pain. Scott was a qualified carpenter, and plagued only with a heroin habit, not the mental disabilities of Stephen. In my opinion, he had a chance of a future, making his death harder to swallow. There must, however, have been an underlying reason, for him to keep re-using.

I thought tragedy was behind me, and as famously said: "Life goes on." Bereavement is a process: "You don't get over it, you get on with it." I'm never going to be without the odd hiccup, having just paid £400 for my back fence to be replaced. The wind had been so severe, blowing it down, breaking both the panels and posts. What with all our trauma, it's hard to believe myself and Brian look 10 years younger than our ages, which I credit to good genes and healthy eating. I had become slightly obsessed with keeping my insides and outsides healthy, intensely reading the back label of everything I bought.

At midnight, we heard the most almighty bang. It was so alarming, I felt too scared to go outside and see. After unlocking the door and venturing out, the sight before us was catastrophe. A mini-van had ploughed through our front garden, narrowly missing the house, but destroying everything else in its path. It had veered over the pavement, skimming the neighbour's fence before driving straight through our metal double gates. The damage it caused clearly showed the speed at which it impacted, approximately 30-40 miles an hour.

The wired fence was mangled, the grass ripped up, and the flowers crushed, the van just abandoned on what was left of the lawn. Brian was an avid gardener, spending hours planting and pruning roses, it was his only hobby and release from the pressures of everyday life.

The neighbours each side emerged and the group of us were shell-shocked. The police were called, and it was early established that the vehicle was stolen from a disability centre. They tried to trace the culprits to no avail, as they had scarpered into the night. Once daylight came, the true scene was revealed, and it was like an abyss. The van's insurance was null due to the vehicle being stolen, so I would have to forfeit the cost myself. The bill totalled £1,100, not to mention the man-hours of work needed to reinstate the garden. Was this just another case of bad luck or was it something more sinister? I have my own suspicions that it was related to a revenge attack from Wagner.

Perhaps there is life after death, but I personally am not superstitious, and believe that once you're dead, you're dead. However, strange things do occur, which cannot be denied and there is no explanation. Michelle said written in biro on her dressing table were the words: "Jordy Nexus Ellis," in Stephen's handwriting. It just appeared and had not been there the previous night. I dismissed it as total rubbish, putting it down to her imagination, but was speechless after observing it for myself. She proceeded to investigate what these words mean by typing them into the Internet, which then directed her to Facebook. The profile photo was of a man with his head and face on fire, which I can only describe is how you would envisage hell. As disturbing as it was I brushed it off as though it meant nothing and had no bearing to my life.

It was now February 2012. I hadn't visited a doctor for years, but after the recent string of disasters I got a little run down. I had a cackle in my throat which was not clearing on its own accord, so felt it was time to get checked out. The GP examined me with his stethoscope and found nothing untoward. I went away quite happy, with a common cold; after all, it was winter.

However, six weeks later the cackle remained, coupled with some chestiness; so, I returned to the surgery. This time I was seen by a locum who made me uncomfortable, as I prefer doctors fully aware of my medical history. I'm sure they are equally as qualified; it's just self-preference. I was prescribed a Ventolin inhaler, the same used by asthma patients, which I knew was of no use but went along with it.

As expected, it proved fruitless as I didn't know how to use gadgets, even struggling with the remote control. No surprises when there was no improvement, after a week, leading me to return to the doctor. My daughters also complained my skin had a tinge of yellowness and fatigue, but I was unaware of its relevance. Two weeks of antibiotics were given to treat a chest infection, and I felt relief this would be wrapped up.

Still not too concerned when after the fortnight there was no difference, a second dose of stronger medication was prescribed, fearing pneumonia. A Russian doctor tended me, asking my symptoms, which was mainly chestiness and sporadic lower back pain. He prescribed further medication but said he was not ruling out lung cancer. I found his suggestion absurd as I did not nor never had smoked in my life. I persevered, but the symptoms persisted even after completing the course, leaving me frustrated. It was over a month now, and the girls were questioning my care, but I couldn't undermine a practitioner's judgement.

My back pain was increasing; so, I had to use the trolley as a crutch whilst browsing the aisles at the supermarket. I shuffled along, letting it take my whole weight. Usually we walked the 30 minutes home, pulling my little domestic trolley behind, but now got a taxi, which I normally see as money wasting. £30 worth of groceries could be crammed into this trolley, which is a godsend as opposed to heavy carrier bags, with plastic handles digging into your palms. That Saturday afternoon, a chronic pain shot up my back, bringing tears to my eyes, and it landed me in A&E. A thorough examination was carried out, which included stretches and physical movements, to identify the cause.

The doctor's verdict was there was no underlying reason for the pain and it bore no relation to my wheezing. Pain killers were provided and were to be used alongside my deep heat cream. I had resorted to rubbing this in nightly, as the aches were hindering even the small amount of sleep I managed.

I was constantly being fobbed off, and my illness not investigated, now into April. I insisted, not the professionals, for a CT scan, as I wanted to clear the blockage that was on my airways. The results were divulged quickly that a shadow was on my lung and the suspected pneumonia was now fact. Struggling to breathe was disabling me, and I had to boycott the gym. Completely fed up as three months had lingered without cure, I demanded an MRI scan, the most detailed.

It was now 11th May 2012, and instead of the procedural two-week wait for my results, I received a call the very next morning. It was requested I go straight to the surgery, raising alarm bells. Still not taking it seriously, Brian remained in the waiting area whilst I went into the room alone. I sat down bewildered, unprepared for the news that was delivered so bluntly. "I am so sorry, you have lung cancer that has spread, and the prognosis is not good."

What? How could this be happening? I had to repeat the diagnosis many times before it would register. My face went as white as a ghost. How could she not have suggested I be accompanied, to receive such devastating news? This was insensitive and enhanced that I was just another person with cancer. I walked home unable to comprehend the situation, but nausea soon overcame me. The girls immediately came round, and we all sat and cried in disbelief. Was this the hell Jordy Nexus Ellis was warning us of?

We are a tenacious family, remaining optimistic and ready to fight. I knew with cancer that time is of the essence, and I needed treatment rapidly. My mind was racing and looking for reasons on how I could have got this. I remembered my own father who died of this very same disease, although there were differentiating factors in our lifestyle.

I must have his genes, as cancer was rife on his side of the family, with many members deceased in their 50s. This included my cousin,

Peter, who suffered a quick death from prostate cancer at 50, dying before both his parents.

Disgusted with the NHS, I wasn't prepared to wait a further two weeks to be informed how advanced it was. The thought of eating food made me feel sick, but I could ill afford not to as I only just realised how thin I was. The cancer had been eating away at me before my very eyes and I never noticed. Now, in a state of panic and unable to breathe due to anxiety, I decided to plant myself at A&E, knowing they wouldn't turn me away.

After a multitude of tests, I was transferred to a private room on the ward, then a young doctor came to my bedside with scan photos under his arm. I asked: "Am I going to die?" Holding my hand, his response was very sensitive, and in a soft voice said: "Well, we are all going to die." My lung cancer was "incurable," which is the new word for "terminal," as it had spread to my liver and bones. My time on this Earth ranged from six months to a year, depending on how I responded to treatment. Was Stephen an angel calling me from up above because he couldn't be without me? Whilst admitted, the build-up of fluid on my chest was drained, filling three litre tubes. This procedure was painful and had to be repeated a few times during my illness.

I was in hospital for the next three days and unable to accept what I had been told. During this time, my daughters stayed with Brian to support him, all still shell-shocked and unable to imagine life without me. They had to dose themselves up on my prescribed sleeping tablets, raiding the stash in my bedside cabinet.

Back home after being discharged, I answered the door to a beautiful bouquet of flowers, arranged by my girls. Amongst all my pain, this uplifted me, bringing tears of emotion.

Cancer is an emotional rollercoaster, and bad news is usually followed by some good. Biopsy results confirmed it wasn't lung but breast cancer, which is more susceptible to treatment and changing my life expectancy to many years. Despite being stage 4, the worst, consultants were hopeful the tumour could be shrunk and kept at bay with intervals of chemo. Relief is an understatement, and maybe those prayers in the hospital chapel had been answered. It was positive news in that it wasn't a return of the breast cancer I had at 46, but a primary one, and easier to contain than secondary. My first chemotherapy dose was on 27th June 2012 and I greeted it with mixed emotions, both excitement and dread. I was now in the driving seat to control this disease but the memories of violently throwing up came flooding back.

The environment was impersonal, playing down the seriousness of the illness, with a conveyor belt of patients, varying in age, attached intravenously to machines. Some even sat reading books whilst the drug cocktail ran through their bodies. My session lasted three hours before being sent home with a variety of anti-sickness and steroid tablets. That night I had no side effects, but the following day nausea set in, and as evening approached I felt so rough. I was vomiting so severely I was choking on the stuff, which in turn led me to fit. I was out of it.

Brian called an ambulance which rushed me directly to intensive care. What the hell was going on? I only had a dose of chemo, which thousands of people do every day. Apparently, I had an allergic reaction to one of the three drugs, causing the sodium in my blood to drop to a dangerously low level. This happens to one in every 10,000 people; of course, I had to be that one!

The family were told my chances of survival were virtually nil and at best I would be brain damaged, due to oxygen starvation when fitting. Doctors implied the kindest course of action was to switch off the life support, but my daughters flat-out refused, and a verbal battle ensued. Instead, they placed a white feather on my forehead which is a "good luck" symbol, and clung to their faith and hope. I was being kept alive by the tube of oxygen inserted down my throat. This procedure can only be sustained under sedation as if awake, the natural reaction is to pull it out.

Days of deliberating with staff resulted in a tracheotomy being performed, meaning a hole was cut in my throat. This would accommodate the tube and I could be conscious. I was brought round, without any brain damage, shocking medics. Being bed ridden for even a short period causes the muscles in your body to waste away. I was, therefore, left with the task of learning to walk again down the hospital corridors. After three weeks of physical rehabilitation, I was discharged, but it was no easy feat. I still didn't have the ability to climb the stairs; so, undignified as it was, I had to urinate in a bucket. I didn't always make it, as my movement was slow, and ended up wetting myself. My throat wound was still sore and didn't look too pleasant, relying on a district nurse to change the dressing, daily. Sometimes they would turn up, and sometimes they wouldn't, which left me open to infection.

I felt handicapped, riddled with medication, and now understanding the term: "If you don't have your health, you don't have anything." All the lengths I had gone to for good health made me question if it was worthwhile. The Macmillan Nurse reassured me, saying the cancer could have struck much earlier, but I had staved it off for even perhaps a decade due to a healthy diet. I was still weak and had to regain my strength before I was allowed a second dose of alternative chemotherapy. The thought of being left untreated for longer than necessary did faze me, but it was out of my hands.

The first dose I had, despite the consequences, should have done something, and I held onto that thought. Alone on the bus after running errands, I stole a few moments to acknowledge I've got cancer, an attacking force inside of me. When first diagnosed, it's a whirlwind of doctors, hospitals and chasing hope, so all reality gets lost.

CHAPTER SIXTEEN

My sister, Anna, and her husband, Trevor, who lived in Cyprus, were coming to stay. Falling in love with the country after a two-week holiday, it's where they decided to lay their hat. He was made redundant from his unskilled job of 20 years, and thought it cheaper to live abroad whilst awaiting his pension to mature. His employers called him "Mr. Unapproachable." When an opportunity arose to end his contract, they took it. I didn't need this right now, but it was a yearly tradition, and their flights were already booked.

We weren't close but were family, and as we have gotten older, it's the best our relationship has been. She felt drawn to me for someone to speak to as the pair of them didn't mix, despite an ex-pats club being nearby. They were shy, wanting to talk but not knowing what to say, also the cost for joining deterred them. We alternated phone calls every Sunday at 6 pm on the dot, with me dominating the whole conversation. To the question of what had they been up to, I received the same response: "Oh, just the usual." One week she would be on the end, and the following week him, which I dreaded as he tended to grunt. Out of frustration I reduced the length of the call from 20 minutes to seven minutes over the months.

The visit was hard work due to extra cooking, shopping, and more bed linen to launder. They were very selfish, expecting to be waited on with the offer of washing up unheard of. They were in their late 50s, having met each other 28 years ago after he placed an advert in the lonely-hearts column. A perfect match as both were frugal and childless through her choice, although he did stress in the early days a desire for one.

She just wasn't maternal never once making a fuss over my kids when they were small. Their meanness drove Brian around the bend as they lived like paupers yet had hundreds of thousands in the bank. Their philosophy was to have something for nothing, believing it was their human right. We hadn't always seen eye-to-eye over the years as Brian's drunken babbling irritated them.

Rather than get a taxi to the airport, or park their own car, they would lug suitcases on foot the 40-minute distance. They denied themselves a variety of foods, living on the same meal every evening: potatoes, cabbage and chicken legs. The chicken legs, however, were soon omitted from the plate due to the cost. This went out the window, at mine, eating everything in sight because they weren't paying.

A British newspaper in Cyprus is two euros, so Trevor would rather fish one out of the bin. He would read it with a magnifying glass to avoid the price of glasses. This only caused further damage as his eyesight deteriorated, being told he would eventually contract glaucoma. Their only other source of entertainment was to watch Greek TV as they refused to pay for a satellite dish. They couldn't understand what was being said, but the pictures must have occupied them.

Brian's anger was understandable, but wanting to keep the peace, I banned him drinking when in their company; otherwise, the truth would come blurting out. As the week progressed, a new toilet roll had to be replaced daily, which was baffling. What could they be using it for? Stashing them to take a few rolls back? When the coast was clear, we searched their suitcase, but they weren't stuffed with toilet rolls, just our old newspapers. I challenged him for an explanation. "Trevor, I am not having a go at you but what are you doing with these toilet rolls? Blowing your nose, wiping your bum, what?" He emphasised it was for his nose. I recounted the incident at Stephen's bedsit, and feared my own toilet would get blocked from flushing such large amounts. It was agreed he now place the tissue in a bag, but in all the confusion he was also bagging his defecated tissue.

When living in the UK, he asked Stephen for adult porn, who then supplied him with DVDs. He must have watched them in secret after Anna went to bed. I don't think she liked sex as their sleeping arrangements always consisted of twin beds, rather than a double.

As time drew to a close, they departed for a week's stay with Trevor's sister in Bristol. She would drive down and collect them from the house, rather than insist they do the under-an-hour train journey. However, their grief over Stephen's death was genuine and they were truly upset. They would regularly light a candle for him at their local Cypriot church.

I was now three months into my chemotherapy, with no side effects other than the usual hair loss. The steroids built up my weight as they increased my appetite; I was eating everything in sight. It's the heaviest I'd ever been and no wonder. After opening a box of Milk Tray all to myself, guilt set in, and I quickly sealed the lid back down with layers of sellotape, barring me having anymore.

People commented how healthy I looked and complimented by my wig, which I only wore when I went out, leaving my head bare indoors. Unfortunately, steroids prevent you from sleeping, so having chronic insomnia any way only made it worse. I didn't feel tired but psychologically knew the body wasn't getting enough sleep to recharge. For years, I'd spend hours laying there desperate to fall off but couldn't, eventually doing so around 5 am to be awake again by 8 am.

I tried various methods to stamp it out, taking both over-the-counter and prescribed sleeping tablets. They stopped working after a while as my body became immune to them, as only being designed for short-term use. I even followed a plan of going to bed and getting up at the same time every day, regardless of how you sleep in between. Preventing early nights and sleeping in late to catch up, re-programmes your body clock. I kept dozing off on the settee whilst reading the newspaper; so, I never gave it a proper chance. Maybe I didn't have a sleep problem, and it was anxiety that was stopping me sleeping.

It was late November 2012, and wanting to experience the Christmas spirit in London, we arranged afternoon tea in Mayfair. Accompanied by the girls, we were treating ourselves at £48 each, to eat to our hearts' content. My attempts to hide the price from Brian failed, who ranted: "Christ that's half my pension!" We did it in style being met at the door by a butler dressed in top hat and tails, fulfilling a wish. It was a wonderful outing. My only complaint was that my legs felt unsteady, presumably the aftermath from intensive care.

Exactly a year earlier, we took the tube to Camden to pay our respects to the late Amy Winehouse, lost to substance dependency. Hearing her name bought a lump to my throat, a very talented young lady with an incredible voice. At the tree adjacent to her home we lit a candle and read the heartfelt messages left from around the world.

The use of my legs was deteriorating daily, and I was also mildly confused when absorbing basic information. At first, doctors associated my confusion to my medication, but a consultant suspected otherwise and arranged a brain scan. Treatment was working in my organs, shrinking the tumour. However, photos of my skull showed the cancer had travelled in my blood up to my brain. Why wasn't my head scanned initially with my body to detect this earlier, as it was now a mass? A medical practitioner should have cottoned on immediately when I raised my leg and mental inabilities. I always prided myself on my sharp mind, but the cancer had even stolen that from me.

Too wobbly to be sent home, I remained in the rehabilitation unit, awaiting a decision on the next stage. It was a two-storey building set aside from the main hospital and designed to give a higher level of care. A general ward was too dangerous as I was liable for a fall and having no hair on my head gave less protection. My oncologist appointment materialised a week later, and in this time my limbs and thinking were diminishing.

Most of the chocolates in my large box of Dairy Milk had been eaten, obviously not by me, as I now needed to be fed. The other inpatients were too weak to move unassisted, so could only have been consumed by the staff. Vulnerability had left me exposed, but it was not unsurprising as care was invisible and the section poorly managed. An auxiliary nurse was being rough when aiding me to the toilet, but she was caught red-handed when the family entered unexpected.

The use of a wheelchair was needed to attend my assessment with Dr. Clarke, the same gentleman who treated my first cancer 20 years prior. The standard reflex tests on my hands and feet proved, in his judgement, I was worthy of radiotherapy in Oxford. My inner strength fought for anything offering a longer life. I was desperate to live. It was the festive season, causing many delays with the NHS transport to Oxford; so, the girls were to borrow a car. This was later forbidden as I was classified unfit and only to be handled by professionals.

Since both their marriages had collapsed, the girls no longer owned a vehicle. Two lengthy relationships, 15 years apiece, now were over, but they were always strained anyway, and I didn't realise. Feeling trapped, legally bound to mortgages and reliant on the husbands' wages prolonged the situation. Perhaps if I hadn't been so preoccupied with Stephen, I would have registered it and helped. It's never too late, but sacrifices have to be made, so they discarded their houses and moved into rented accommodation with the children.

Another obstacle was put before me as the norovirus was spreading, and Oxford refused to admit any patients until the all-clear. Radiotherapy was delayed for another seven days, which can only have negative consequences. Due to all the waiting, I was now confined to bed with safety bars and in a coma-like state. The hospice was now mentioned as an option, but the family refused, insisting they adhere to the original plan. They felt I had been left to rot unnecessarily, and they wouldn't give up without trying.

An ambulance drove me to the Churchill Hospital, where my condition was monitored. To receive radiotherapy, I had to be alert and able to lay unattended; otherwise, it's unsafe. My steroid dosage was also increased to stimulate as much as possible. Dr. Debenham was now responsible for my care. He made me very comfortable, but sadly knew it was too late. Encouraged to fight, Brian and the girls activated my mind and limbs by quizzing me on their names and dates of birth, which I recalled. There was a pot of red liquid on my bedside tray, which Brian fed me, presuming it was jelly. It was only when the nurse revealed it was actually mouthwash that a hint of laughter was bought to our heartache.

The next day, the grandchildren were bought up on the double-decker bus because they wanted to visit me. When arriving at my bedside, they were shocked to see how ill I was. Staff relaxed the rules on this occasion, allowing all five of them in at once.

Unfortunately, the cancer was progressing. I was barely able to stay awake, and my breathing was strained. For hours, they tried to revive me by calling my name: "Marilyn, Marilyn." I wanted to respond but couldn't. In the early hours of 5th January 2013, I drew my last breath and died alone at age 67 in bed number 50. Coincidentally, Stephen died at flat number 50. So, we were connected in life and death.

Stephen and myself

Epilogue

In the midst of our continuing grief, we have strived on, although it has been emotionally challenging to write this. We believe in fate. It all began with a call from Julie enquiring as to the well-being of her cancer-stricken friend, Marilyn. As Marilyn was too weak to shuffle to the telephone, Michelle intercepted the conversation which led to the birth of *Tenacity*. Prior to this, both families had felt alone in their grief as nobody wanted to listen to the story of drugs. Or, perhaps, we were just the chosen ones.

Michelle always knew we had a story worth telling and was not defeated by the many knock backs she endured from counselling training and placements. Through experiencing Stephen's drug problem first hand, she wanted to utilise her knowledge and understanding to help others struggling with trauma. The three authors met up regularly to build up a rapport, enabling us to share private details. The research of the family history had occurred earlier over several years, not knowing at the time that it would be used for this purpose. Our dream was for the original eBook to become available in paperback, along with a sequel, *Tenacity Continued ...*, which we are currently considering.

The tone is hard-hitting as it resulted in the deaths of Scott and Stephen aged 28 and 31, respectively, both in their prime. Perhaps the course of events even triggered Marilyn's cancer, costing another life and tearing relationships apart. Our aim is to act as a deterrent, in the hope it will awaken people to the dangers of what can lie ahead and empower them with the strength to resist temptation.

We feel the key is to educate throughout schools and colleges, before youth falls into this trap. Support networks play a huge part in feeding our information through to the different levels of treatment and recovery. Our goal is for our work to be recognised and used in their teachings. It equips both professionals and patients with a portal into our trials and tribulations. Knowledge is power. So, perhaps lessons can be learnt from what we did or didn't do.

Marilyn Ann Cowell did not die in vain. She left her legacy, which will be carried forward in this war on addiction. She was an inspirational lady with a heart of gold, and she held a presence wherever she went. Although her death was untimely, her life was lived with significance and impact. She was unique. We dedicate *Tenacity* to all the mothers and fathers who live this nightmare every single day. You are the true heroes!

Our heartfelt thanks go out to Joanna Kluessien, Director of Narconon, and Karen Kirby at Broadway Lodge for supporting and believing in our project and moving it forward.

Also we would like to thank Morrisons UK Supermarket chain for their help and support in initially introducing the book to their staff as members of the public.

But most of all a huge thank you goes to Stanley and Joseph for their love belief and support.

About the Authors

I am Julie Rose. I work in mortgages for a large company. Michelle Louise and Sarah Jane Cowell are sisters, the daughters of Marilyn Cowell who died before her story could be told. Michelle and Sarah are customer service assistants in Retail. Since finishing the book, the subject of addiction has taken us to many places within the UK and Holland, including recovery centres, rehabs, and drug seminars. We have met some marvellous dedicated people in the field of addiction and spoken to recovering addicts trying to conquer this disease. We have spread the word by telling our story in local and national newspapers in the UK,
Holland and the US. Among them:

The Oxford Mail UK
The Sunday Express UK
The Swindon Advertiser UK
The Paisley Daily Mail Scotland
The Fleetwood Weekly UK
The Blackpool Gazette UK
Holland's local newspaper 'Contact,' in Zutphen
Sober World, America

We believe that educating the young on the dangers of substance abuse is the key to preventing drug tragedies. Our drug awareness talks started in 2018 to secondary schools in the UK to 13–14-year olds. Our talks within the schools will continue as we tell our story.

Our Aim ...

... Is whenever a young person is in a situation where they are tempted to use drugs, they will remember our story or our talk. That could be the difference between a life of addiction hell, or a bright healthy future.

Thank you for reading our book.

MIX
Paper
FSC® C100212

Printed by Imprimerie Gauvin
Gatineau, Québec